**Hawkeye and the Others Are Operating Again...
and they'll have you in stitches!**

You'll find them here in the quiz book that asks all the questions and gives all the answers about the most beloved show on T.V. After a ten-year love affair, there is so much to be remembered. Here's you[r] [chanc]e to test your recall of Hawkeye's one-liners, H[awkey's on], Winchester's woes and all the rest [of] [the] [MASH] [memor]abilia.

And [how well did you do]
with th[e] [questions on the cover:]

1) Colonel [Blake got a s]hell fragment in his eye, a[nd] [   ] [   ] 3) Sal Viscuso
4) Ottumwa, [Iowa   5)] Colonel Potter   6) A visiting specialist playe[d] by Robert Alda   7) The Statute of Liberty   8) A body cast   9) His teddy bear
10) Just BJ. He was named after his parents: his mother Bea and his father Jay.

They're all inside—Radar, Trapper John, Colonel Blake, BJ, Klinger, Colonel Potter, and *perhaps* some names you may not remember. But you won't know for certain till you take a crack at...

M.A.S.H. TRIVIA THE UNOFFICIAL QUIZ BOOK

It's Just What The Doctor Ordered!

M.A.S.H. TRIVIA
THE UNOFFICIAL
QUIZ BOOK

George St. John

WARNER BOOKS

A Warner Communications Company

To my mother, Delores,
and to my sisters, Leah and Serrie

ACKNOWLEDGEMENTS

My thanks for their help go out to Pam Brickman, Dave Jonasen, Joe Knapp, Charlie McCarthy, Jeff McCarthy, Ellen Meyer, Connie Pinkham, Janet Rindo, Tom Spaeth, Bill Shannon, Bunny Thomson, Dennis Winslow, and Craig Witte. And an especially big thanks to Donald Rindo, Tom Mertes, and my editor, Brian Thomsen.

TABLE OF CONTENTS

Introduction   **xi**

During One Episode (The Early Years)   **1**

Terminology   **15**

During One Episode (The Middle Years)   **17**

The Korean War   **29**

During One Episode (The Later Years)   **31**

During the Final Episode   **47**

The Characters   **51**

Quotations   **59**

The Cast   **61**

MASH: The Book   **67**

Guest Stars   **71**

*M*A*S*H:* The Movie   **77**

Odds & Ends   **81**

THE M*A*S*H Exam   **87**

When I was an undergrad at the University of Wisconsin–Milwaukee, every evening, faithfully, I would go to the second-floor east wing of the Golda Meir Library, ostensibly to study. Quite often, however, I never got around to studying. Instead of writing a brief on Baker *v.* Carr, or reading the assigned chapters in Samuelson's *Economics,* or considering whether or not F. D. R. was a traitor to his class, my friends and I would ask each other trivia questions about M*A*S*H†. My friends were so knowledgeable that it became a challenge for me to come up with better, more interesting questions than the ones they put to me. We quickly advanced from the "What is Colonel Potter's horse's name?" type of questions to "What were Henry's last words?" or "What are Mrs. Potter's measurements?" All of the questions came solely from our memories and the various public materials available to us (e.g. *TV Guide,* magazine articles, interviews from TV talk shows,

†M*A*S*H is a trademark of Twentieth Century-Fox Film Corporation. This book is not connected with or authorized by the trademark owner or any of its licensees.

etc.). We were just a group of fans testing each other on our favorite show. The end results of all my hard studying at U.W.–M. are a Bachelor of Arts degree (I majored in history, class of '82) and this book.

I can almost hear a late night talk show host saying it now: "This book contains every question, every single M*A*S*H trivia question, that anyone could ever think of!" Well, as a particularly derisive guest star for the evening might reply, "You are wrong, latrine breath!" For instance, I'm missing a Colonel Potter question. (It's here somewhere, I'm sure, among all the scraps of paper and napkins upon which I wrote the questions.) But the point is that not every conceivable question is included—just, I hope, the most interesting and challenging questions. Wait a minute, stop the presses! Here it is, my missing Colonel Potter question: "What is the Colonel's hobby?" At any rate, even without that question, I'm sure you'll enjoy *M.A.S.H. Trivia the Unofficial Quiz Book.* There are enough questions to keep you entertained for hours. And don't forget to take our special quiz in the back of the book and find out exactly what your M*A*S*H I.Q. is.

One final note. I love receiving mail. Should you have any comments on the book, please send them to me in care of Warner Books. But I want to hear only the good stuff.

Here's looking up your old address!

George St. John
Milwaukee, Wisconsin
April 1983

P.S. Colonel Potter's hobby is painting.

(The most difficult questions are marked with an asterisk[*].)

M.A.S.H. TRIVIA
THE UNOFFICIAL
QUIZ BOOK

When M*A*S*H made its debut as part of the fall 1972 CBS line-up, the course of the show was still to be decided. The hi-jinx and gore of the original film had to be toned down, with its overall irreverent tone maintained. Also, several major turnovers in the major supporting cast of players were made during the early episodes. Yet, somehow, it all came together.

DURING ONE EPISODE
(The Early Years)

In the very first M*A*S*H episode, Hawkeye held a raffle so that he could raise enough money to send Ho-John to the States . . . .

1. What prize did he give away?

2. Who won the prize?

3. Who drew the winning raffle ticket?

4. Why was Ho-John being sent to the States?

Hawkeye and Trapper had to deal with the black market to obtain some badly needed hydrocortisone . . . .

5. From whom did they acquire the hydrocortisone?

6. What did they have to give up in order to get it?

Hawkeye had a "moose" . . . .

7. What was her name?

8. How did he obtain her?

9. From whom did he obtain her?

A rash of stealing plagues the 4077th, with Hawkeye being the chief suspect . . . .

10. What was stolen from Major Burns?

11. What was stolen from Hot Lips?

12. Who really did the stealing?

13. How did Hawkeye find out who the culprit was?

Henry chose Hawkeye, instead of Burns, to be the 4077th's chief surgeon . . . .

14. What was the name of the General who went to the 4077th to look into Burns's complaint?

15. What was the General's suggestion as to how to deal with Burns?

To keep a beautiful nurse from being transferred out of the 4077th, Trapper agreed to fight in the intercamp boxing tournament . . . .

16. What was the name of the nurse he was fighting for?

17. Who was his opponent?

18. What unit was he from?

19. What was his record?

A chopper pilot wanted to kill Henry, because Henry refused to allow the pilot to go home so that he could straighten out his marriage . . . .

20. What was the pilot's nickname, and what was his real name?

*21. What was his wife's name, and what was her address?

22. What were the four ''accidents'' that befell Henry?

A propaganda film was to be made about the fine work done at the 4077th. Hawkeye and Trapper didn't like the film, so they sabotaged it and made one of their own....

23. Who was the director of the original film?

24. Who provided the film's introduction?

25. What was the title of Hawkeye's and Trapper's film?

26. Who was the narrator of the film?

27. What was to be left of their film after cutting?

Hawkeye drew the short straw and was thus forced to date a lonely, bumbling nurse....

28. Who was the nurse?

29. Why was he forced to date her?

Radar was down in the dumps because he received a "Dear John" record from his girlfriend back home....

30. What was the name of the girl who dumped Radar?

31. What was the name of the guy she dumped Radar for?

*32. Where was the "Dear John" record made?

33. What was the name of the nurse who made Radar forget his troubles?

Hawkeye, Trapper, and Radar created a "captain" so that they could donate supplies to a nearby orphanage....

34. Which orphanage was it?

35. What was the captain's name?

36. Why did Hawkeye choose that particular name?

37. Where was the captain from?

38. In what year was he born?

*39. What were: a) his height? b) his weight? c) his hair color? d) his eye color?

40. What was his religion?

41. What were the names of his parents?

42. What medical school had he attended?

43. How many months back pay did he have coming to him?

44. How did he die?

45. Who was his "replacement"?

Hawkeye, Trapper, and Radar convinced a colonel whose battle casualty rate was too high that he had battle fatigue and should be shipped home for treatment . . . .

46. Who was the colonel?

47. What nervous habit did he have?

48. Where was his tent located?

49. What did they convince him he drank?

Radar wanted to earn his high school diploma via a correspondence course . . . .

50. What was the name of the school and where was it located?

51. Radar was asked a question about the significance of the dates 1776 and 1492. What was his answer?

52. Did he pass the test?

53. Who tested him?

Hawkeye's friend, a journalist, wrote a book on the Korean War, but he never lived to see it published . . . .

54. What was his name?

55. What was the title of his book?

56. Was the title "correct?"

Hawkeye had a pair of long johns which, in the middle of winter, was worth its weight in gold. They went from Hawkeye to Trapper to Radar to the cook to Burns to Hot Lips to Klinger to Father Mulcahy to Henry and, once again, to Hawkeye....

57. How did Trapper lose them to Radar?

58. What did Radar trade them for?

59. How did Klinger get them?

60. What were the long johns "as soft as"?

Burns and Hot Lips both got fed up with Hawkeye's and Trapper's practical jokes (especially the broadcasting of one of their rendezvous over the PA system), and requested a transfer out of the 4077th....

61. Why did Hawkeye and Trapper NOT want them to leave?

62. How did Hawkeye and Trapper keep them from leaving?

After publicly calling Burns incompetent, Hawkeye agonizes when one of his own patients, for no apparent reason, keeps getting worse and worse....

63. Who was the patient?

64. What was wrong with him?

An unexploded bomb landed in the middle of the 4077th's compound, disrupting the broadcast of the Army–Navy football game....

65. Whose bomb was it?

66. Whose job was it to defuse the bomb?

*67. What were the markings on the bomb?

68. What happened when it exploded?

69. Who won the Army–Navy game, and what was the final score?

Everyone at the 4077th celebrated because they thought the war was over....

70. Hawkeye tore up $1500 in poker IOUs. How did he say he would recoup the money?

71. What did Hawkeye write in Radar's scrapbook?

While a USO show was going on, Henry was miserable because he couldn't be with his wife, who was giving birth to their baby....

*72. How much did his son weigh, and how long (in inches) was he?

73. What was the name of the comedian who entertained the troops?

Radar, in filling out the weekly report, described the antics at the 4077th....

74. What was the name of the nurse who was attacked in OR by a Chinese POW and who was under the "personal" supervision of Hawkeye?

75. What did the Chinese say that Father Mulcahy mistakenly repeated to the POW, and what did it really mean?

General Clayton assigned an incognito psychiatrist to the 4077th to determine if the unit should be broken up and the men reassigned....

76. Who was the psychiatrist?

An inept North Korean pilot tried at the same time every day to bomb an ammo dump located near the 4077th....

77. What nickname was given to the pilot?

*78. How long had the pilot been trying to blow up the ammo dump?

79. Who won the daily lottery on how close to the dump the bomb would land?

80. Why was it decided to try to shoot down the pilot?

Complete with the destruction of evidence, a disappearing witness, and censored mail, the U.S. tried to cover up the accidental bombing of a South Korean village....

81. What was the name of the village?

82. To whom did Hawkeye and Trapper report the incident, and where was that person transferred to?

83. Hawkeye wanted a friend of his dad's, U.S. Senator Baxter, to help. Why couldn't the Senator help them?

84. As partial compensation, the bombed village was given something that no other village in Southeast Asia had. What was it?

Hawkeye, after three days of almost nonstop duty, discovered what the war was all about....

85. What did he try to have sent to North Korea, in the hope of ending the war?

Hawkeye and Trapper helped an enlisted man who wanted to marry a Korean girl cut through all of the red tape....

86. What was the name of the soldier who wanted to get married?

87. What was the name of the CID man who investigated the case?

88. How did Hawkeye and Trapper get the CID man to approve the marriage?

Trapper wanted to adopt a small Korean boy . . . .

89. What was the boy's name?

90. Where did the boy wander off to?

91. What was the name of the chopper pilot who rescued the boy?

Henry was put on trial for various things, including giving aid and comfort to the enemy . . . .

92. Who brought the charges against Henry?

93. One of the irregularities cited was a race that the 4077th held on Kentucky Derby Day (one of the entrants was "Bouncing Betty"). What type of race was it?

94. Another irregularity was Radar's selling a certain kind of shoe door-to-door (or tent-to-tent). What kind was it?

95. Who came to the rescue, testifying on Henry's behalf?

In a letter to his dad, Hawkeye described all that was going on at the 4077th. Among other things, there was a soldier who wanted to be given the "right color blood," and a home movie from Henry's wife . . . .

96. What was the name of the soldier who wanted "white" blood?

97. How did Henry say he met his wife?

*98. Who was the Blakes' next-door neighbor, and what did he do for a living?

Hawkeye and Trapper decided that they needed an incubator . . . .

99. How did they go about getting one?

The 4077th was attacked by a single sniper....

100. Who did the sniper mistakenly believe he was attacking?

101. How did they finally get rid of him?

During the weekly officers' poker game, Henry had to help get Radar out of a jam after Radar hit an old Korean man with his jeep....

102. What was the accident victim's nickname?

103. When Radar hit the old man, what sound did the accident make: a "thump" or a "thud"?

*104. How much did they give to the man as a pay-off?

Hawkeye and Trapper saved the life of a general's son....

105. Who was the general?

106. What was the son's name?

107. What did the general give to them as a reward?

108. What concession to "military rules" was made?

Henry fell in love with a much younger woman....

109. What was her name?

110. Where was she from?

111. How old was she?

*112. What college had she attended?

113. What did she "give" to Hawkeye that he said he'd never forget?

Hawkeye was in desperate need of a pair of boots and was willing to make any sort of deal to get them....

114. What was the dentist's name, and what did he want?

9

115. Who was the birthday cake for, and who was to supply it?

116. What was the name of the nurse Radar wanted to date, and what did she want before she would go out with him?

117. At what point did the deals collapse?

118. What did Hawkeye wear after he was unable to get the boots?

*119. What was Hawkeye's boot size?

Burns wanted to slap a dishonorable discharge on a wounded soldier who admitted to being a homosexual . . . .

120. What was the soldier's name?

121. How did Hawkeye and Trapper get Burns to drop the discharge?

Hawkeye tricked Burns into buying stock in a fictitious company . . . .

122. What was the name of the company?

Hawkeye, Trapper, Burns, Radar, and Klinger traveled deep inside enemy lines to carry out an exchange of wounded prisoners . . . .

123. Where did this exchange take place?

*124. What was the enemy officer's name?

125. What medical school had he attended?

Klinger got married via shortwave radio . . . .

126. Who was his bride?

127. Who married them?

128. What did Klinger wear?

A famous general died in Hot Lips's tent, but the general's aide wanted it to appear as though the general had died a hero in combat . . . .

129. Who was the deceased general?

130. Who was the general's aide?

While Burns was buying two pearl necklaces, the real one intended for his wife and the fake intended for Hot Lips, Trapper was winning and then losing a big poker pot . . . .

131. According to Hot Lips, how can you tell real pearls from fake?

132. What did Trapper use for his ante when he won the big pot?

133. What happened to the money?

Hawkeye, as Officer of the Day, had to treat several Korean LIPs, all of whom had the same name . . . .

134. What was the name they all used?

Harry Morgan (before he became Colonel Potter) played a crazy, by-the-book general . . . .

135. What was his name?

136. What song did he sing at Hawkeye's court martial?

137. What eventually happened to him?

Army Intelligence reported that North Korea was planning to invade the 4077th by air. Fearing for their safety, the nurses were temporarily transferred to a safer locale . . . .

138. Where were they transferred to?

139. When the air "invasion" did come, what happened?

Radar tricked Henry into shipping a lamb to the States so that it wouldn't wind up as Easter dinner....

140. Where did the 4077th get the lamb?

141. What was the lamb's name?

142. What type of discharge was it given?

143. How was the lamb replaced?

Trapper almost got his discharge....

144. Why?

145. Why wasn't he sent home?

General MacArthur paid a visit to the 4077th....

146. What did Klinger dress as?

While Henry was on leave, Burns, as second in command, banned alcohol. He asked Father Mulcahy to give a "fire and brimstone" sermon on the evils of drink....

*147. Which Biblical verse did Father Mulcahy unsuccessfully try to quote?

148. Why did he mess it up?

Hawkeye hit Burns and was placed under house (or tent) arrest for striking a superior officer....

149. According to Trapper, what actually happened?

*150. What were the contents of the prisoner kit that Hawkeye was given by Father Mulcahy?

151. What was the name of the nurse who accused Burns of rape?

Hawkeye, tired of the usual food, decided to send out to Chicago for an order of ribs....

152. What were the two foods he was most tired of eating?

153. From what restaurant did he get the ribs?

*154. Before he could get the ribs, Hawkeye had to make a few long distance phone calls. What was the telephone number of the Dearborn Street Station?

*155. What was the telephone number of the restaurant?

156. What was the name of the woman (she was one of Trapper's old friends) who shipped the package to Korea?

157. What reason did Trapper give her for them needing the ribs?

158. What was the name of the sergeant who demanded a portion of the ribs?

*159. Where was he from?

160. What did Hawkeye forget to order?

A doctor who was visiting Korea was supposed to perform a new and delicate operation on a patient. He was unable to do so, however, because he was a lush . . . .

161. What was his name?

162. What operation was it?

Hawkeye said that Captain Adam Casey was the finest surgeon he had ever seen. The only catch: Casey was an impostor . . . .

163. What were Casey's real name and rank?

164. What else did he pass himself off as?

165. As what did he leave the camp?

While Hawkeye and Trapper were helping an orderly visit his pregnant wife, they were also trying to prevent a soldier from marrying a local "business" girl . . . .

166. What was the soldier's name?

167. What was the name of the girl he wanted to marry?

168. Why was he unable to marry her?

169. What did Mr. Kwan, the orderly, name his son?

Hawkeye, Hot Lips, and Klinger were sent to an aid station under heavy fire at the front....

170. How did Hawkeye happened to get picked?

171. What were the radio code names of Klinger at the aid station, and of Radar at the 4077th?

Henry got his discharge....

172. What was the title of this episode?

173. What farewell present did Hawkeye, Trapper, and Radar give to Henry?

174. "I'm afraid just a handshake won't do it." Who said that line, and how did the two bid each other farewell?

175. What were Henry's last words, and to whom were they spoken?

176. How and where did Henry die?

177. Who broke the news of Henry's death to the 4077th?

TERMINOLOGY

What do the following M*A*S*H medical and military terms mean:

1. M.A.S.H
2. OR?
3. OD?
4. Triage?
5. Aorta?
6. Latrine?
7. Bug out?
8. Hemostat?
9. Stat?
10. LIP?
11. Moose?

12. Hemorraghic fever?
13. Catgut?
14. 3-0 silk?
15. Section 8?
16. Cardiac massage?
17. Pentothal?
18. Lap sponge?
19. Aneurysm?
20. Thoracic?
21. Incubator?
22. Meatball surgery?
23. Bowel resection?
24. Peritonitis?
25. Metzenbaum scissors?
26. Hydrocortisone?
27. Irrigation?
28. Adrenaline?
29. Hypothermia?
30. Anesthesiologist?

The Middle Years saw a turnover in the command of the 4077th, the exiting of Trapper John, and the addition of BJ Hunnicut. The show itself went through some changes, too, with the advent of such nontraditional episodes as Hawkeye's show-long monologue in the episode "Hawkeye," and an episode shot entirely in black-and-white documentary fashion entitled "The Interview."

DURING ONE EPISODE
(The Middle Years)

While Hawkeye was on R 'n' R, Trapper went home. He was replaced by Captain BJ Hunnicut. And Colonel Potter arrived at the 4077th to take over command....

1. What farewell "message" did Trapper leave with Radar for Hawkeye?

2. What airport did Trapper depart from and BJ arrive at?

3. What were BJ's first words to Frank Burns?

*4. Exactly when (time and date) did Colonel Potter arrive at the 4077th?

It was Colonel and Mrs. Potter's wedding anniversary....

5. What present did Radar give to the Colonel?

6. What present did Majors Burns and Houlihan give to him?

Because of a bureaucratic mix-up, Hawkeye was declared to be dead....

7. Who was the person assigned the job of getting Hawkeye's body?

8. Why was Hawkeye unable to notify his dad that he was alive?

9. When Hawkeye finally was able to get through to his dad, what did he ask him for?

A chopper pilot with diabetes didn't want to be grounded, because he was in the running for an award....

10. What was his name, and his nickname?

11. What was his favorite drink?

12. What little trick did he have which enabled him to get his favorite drink for free?

*13. How many wounded did he recover with his chopper?

14. Who eventually did win the award?

It was BJ's turn to write a letter home. He told his wife of an attempt to set a world record for having the largest number of people in a jeep. And he told her of Father Mulcahy's agony in being forced by the division chaplain to tell a soldier's parents that their son was fine, when in fact he was still in danger....

15. How many people did they squeeze into the jeep?

16. Who was the division chaplain?

17. What did the other chaplains refer to him as?

18. What was the soldier's name?

*19. What did the soldier's father do for a living?

Hawkeye and BJ treated a few patients off the record....

20. What was the name of the American colonel who got a shot of penicillin for his VD?

21. How did he repay Hawkeye and BJ?

22. Also treated was a British officer. What was his name?

23. What was his problem?

24. What was the fee?

A bunch of kids sought refuge at the 4077th after their orphanage was bombed, and Burns showed off his newly acquired Purple Heart....

25. What was the name of the nurse who ran the orphanage?

26. What did one little girl call Klinger?

27. What bedtime story did BJ tell?

28. What "bedtime story" did Colonel Potter tell?

29. What did Burns do in order to receive a Purple Heart?

Their bus broke down, leaving Colonel Potter, Hawkeye, BJ, Burns, and Radar lost in the middle of nowhere....

30. Where did Burns, on the walkie-talkie, say they were located?

31. To kill time, they talked about the "first time that love conquered all." Who was Colonel Potter's first love?

32. Who was Burns's first love?

33. He said that they had met at a debate. What was the topic?

A wounded officer believed that he was Jesus Christ....

34. Who, in fact, was the officer?

35. What state was he from?

36. Where had he gone to college?

*37. How many missions had he flown?

While Burns was lying in post-op with a severe fever, a "Soldier of the Month" contest was held . . . .

38. Believing that he was close to death, Burns made out his will. What did he leave to Hot Lips?

39. What specific kind of fever did he have?

40. Who competed in the "Soldier of the Month" contest?

41. What was the prize?

42. Klinger was asked the question, "What famous Civil War hero said, 'Damn the torpedos!'?" What was his answer?

43. Who won the contest?

As Radar was writing a letter home to his mom, Colonel Potter was getting wounded and Hawkeye was conducting a foot inspection . . . .

44. Radar said he was writing the letter slowly. Why?

45. How was Potter wounded?

46. Where was he wounded?

47. Why did Burns refuse to allow his feet to be inspected?

Radar was accused of stealing a fancy gun which was the property of a wounded colonel . . . .

48. What was the name of the colonel who owned this collector's piece?

49. Can you describe the gun?

50. Who was the real culprit?

Potter was about to become a grandfather . . . .

  51. What did the Colonel's son do for a living?

  52. What was his daughter-in-law's name?

  53. What was his granddaughter's name?

*54. How much did she weigh at birth?

Radar discovered that Colonel Potter loved tomato juice, and he wanted Requisition Officer Burns to order some . . . .

  55. What did Burns want before he would order the tomato juice?

  56. What was Potter's response to the tomato juice?

After being injured in a jeep accident, Hawkeye talked on endlessly with a Korean family who didn't understand a word he was saying . . . .

*57. Hawkeye said the Pierce family arrived in Maine at what time?

  58. While in med school, at what restaurant did Hawkeye like to eat whitefish?

  59. Who did Hawkeye say was the head of his med school?

  60. When Hawkeye returned, what did he give to each member of the family?

While Burns was selling the 4077th's garbage, Hawkeye was unable to perform sexually, and he had a run-in with a colonel who insisted on retrieving the bodies of dead soldiers . . . .

  61. Who was the nurse with whom Hawkeye had the "BIG couldn't"?

  62. Who was the colonel?

63. What did Hawkeye do with the garbage he bought from Burns?

Potter asked Hawkeye and BJ to be nice to Burns while Hot Lips was away . . . .

64. After Burns passed out from drinking too much, Hawkeye and BJ put a toe-tag on him. What did the tag say?

65. Where did Burns wind up?

While Colonel Potter was away and Burns was in command, Hawkeye allegedly committed mutiny . . . .

*66. What was the date of the "mutiny"?

67. Who was the judge at the trial?

68. One of the steps leading up to the mutiny was Zale's losing some money in a poker game. How much did he lose, and where was the money hidden?

69. What really happened at the time of the alleged mutiny?

The only woman Hawkeye ever seriously considered marrying stopped by the 4077th . . . .

*70. What was her name?

71. What was her husband's name, and what did he do for a living?

A war correspondent interviews members of the 4077th . . . .

72. Who was the interviewer?

73. What was the one thing that Father Mulcahy said moved him the most?

74. Hawkeye said one thing he hated was that almost everything was colored green. What two things weren't green?

75. What was different about this episode?

Margaret came back from Tokyo with the news that she was engaged to be married . . . .

76. Who was her fiance?

*77. What had been his standing in his class at West Point?

78. Who did Burns go out and arrest as spies?

Hawkeye, via some bad nightmares and sleepwalking, returns to a time when life was simpler: his childhood . . . .

79. When he was a kid, Hawkeye said he was one of the "Three Musketeers." Who were the other two?

*80. Who had been the principal of his school?

81. In one of his nightmares, he saw a friend going down a hill on a sled heading straight toward a tree. What was the name of the hill?

82. When he was sleepwalking, he thought Radar was one of his childhood buddies. Which one?

83. What sport did he play in his sleep?

Radar was promoted to Second Lieutenant . . . .

84. Who was responsible for his promotion?

85. Why was he promoted?

86. When Colonel Potter checked to see if the promotion was legit, what reason was given for the promotion?

While Hawkeye was blinded from a stove explosion, Burns tried to clean up by betting on baseball games for which he already knew the results . . . .

87. What was the name of the doctor who treated Hawkeye?

*88. To get even with Burns, Hawkeye did the play-by-play on a fake game. Who were the two teams, and what was the final score, in Hawkeye's version?

*89. What was the final score in the actual game?

BJ was sold a watch with no insides . . . .

90. Who sold him the watch?

91. Under what pretense was it sold?

An overweight general who smoked cigars and had high blood pressure wanted Hawkeye to be his personal physician . . . .

92. What was his name?

Hot Lips was having a difficult time handling some of her nurses. One, in particular, was confined to quarters. When her husband, a soldier, showed up at the 4077th, Hawkeye and BJ had to come up with a scheme to get the two together . . . .

93. Who was the nurse?

94. What was her husband's name?

Major Freedman wrote a letter "home" . . . .

95. How did he start the letter?

96. In his letter, Freedman described a rash of practical jokes. Who was the culprit?

97. What was the practical joke aimed at Burns and which involved his foxhole?

98. Another incident involved an ambulance driver who was killed when his ambulance crashed. What was his name?

99. Who wrote the letter home to his parents?

While Colonel Potter was away, his horse became sick. And it was up to Hawkeye and BJ to cure her . . . .

100. BJ called his father-in-law for advice on the horse. What was his father's name?

*101. Where did he live?

102. What was wrong with the horse?

103. What did Hawkeye and BJ have to do to her to cure her?

Hawkeye and BJ tried to pass a North Korean surgeon off as a South Korean . . . .

104. What alias did the doctor use?

105. What was his real name?

106. What college had he attended, and what year did he graduate?

Because he had never actually seen fighting, Father Mulcahy was unable to help a soldier who purposely shot himself to get out of combat. He was unable to help the soldier until he received his own baptism under fire . . . .

107. What was the name of the soldier who shot himself?

108. What was the name of the priest both Father Mulcahy and the soldier knew?

109. What exactly did Father Mulcahy do to earn his baptism under fire?

Radar became friends with a soldier who was a former star college football player . . . .

110. What were his name and rank?

111. What position had he played?

112. What state was he from?

113. What operation was performed on him?

114. What was his response to the operation?

*115. In the end, how did he decide to deal with it?

One of Colonel Potter's old friends needed some combat time in order to get a promotion. Unfortunately, he turned out to be a disaster as a combat soldier, causing unnecessary casualties. And the 4077th's Ping Pong champ got married . . . .

116. What was the name of Colonel Potter's friend?

117. How much time did the friend need at the front?

118. What was his usual assignment?

119. Who was the groom in the Ping Pong champ marriage?

120. Who was the bride?

121. How did the groom enter the ceremony?

122. What was unusual, to a Western mind, about the Buddhist wedding ceremony?

Radar took a correspondence course in creative writing, and it was Major Burns's birthday . . . .

123. From what school did Radar take this course?

124. Radar asked Burns for an amusing anecdote. What was it?

125. What present did Hawkeye and BJ give to Burns?

126. What was Hawkeye's "last word"?

127. After dropping his creative writing course, what did Radar then decide to take up?

A chopper pilot had a rather profitable side business dealing in war souvenirs, and Klinger's latest escapade involved sitting on top of a pole . . . .

128. Who was the pilot with the souvenir business?

*129. Exactly how long did Klinger sit on top of the pole?

Margaret got married....

130. Who gave away the bride?

131. Who was best man at the ceremony?

132. Where did Margaret get her wedding gown?

133. What did the groom wear?

BJ and Hawkeye found an unfinished crossword puzzle, and, with help from everyone at the 4077th, they were able to complete it. However, they did have a difficult time with a five-letter Yiddish word for bedbug....

134. What is a five-letter Yiddish word for bedbug?

*135. What number clue was it?

136. The crossword puzzle came from what newspaper?

137. What was the name of the friend Hawkeye radioed to for help in solving the puzzle?

138. Where was the friend at the time?

BJ, only one time, was almost unfaithful to his wife....

139. Who was the other woman?

140. What was her problem?

Hawkeye came down with back pain, which was brought on when an "incredibly average" colleague of his was awarded a big medical grant....

141. Who was this "incredibly average" person?

The 4077th got a treat. A classic movie, full of splices, relieved some built-up tension....

142. What movie was it? (Hint: it starred Henry Fonda and Walter Brennan.)

143. According to Colonel Potter, what three things must a movie have in order for it to be considered "great"?

144. Who did Radar do impressions of?

145. When it was BJ's and Hawkeye's turn in the sing-a-long, who did they work on "during the day" and "through the night"?

146. Who did both Colonel Potter and Margaret do impressions of?

The Korean War

1. When did the Korean War begin?

2. Who was the President of the United States at the time?

3. Who was the President of Korea at the time?

4. Which nations fought on the side of the United Nations?

5. On 15 September 1950, General MacArthur, Commander of the UN forces, launched a brilliant amphibious assault which repelled the North Koreans. Where did this landing take place?

6. In fighting in Korea, the United States decided to fight a "limited" war. What is the name of the river separating North Korea from Manchuria that the UN forces were prohibited from fighting to the north of?

7. Why did the United States not want to take the fighting north of that river?

8. War with China "would involve us in the wrong war, at

the wrong place, at the wrong time, and with the wrong enemy." Who said that famous line?

9. What happened on 10 April 1951?

10. Who replaced General MacArthur as Commander of the UN forces?

11. What was Operation "Ripper"?

12. What was Operation "Little Switch"?

13. When did the Korean War finally end?

14. What is the name of the boundary separating North and South Korea?

15. Who was the President of the United States when the war ended?

16. What are the official names of North and South Korea?

17. What are the capitals of North and South Korea?

18. What was the Korean "War" euphemistically called?

19. Roughly, how many Americans were killed and wounded in the Korean War?

20. What incident in January 1968 rekindled bad feelings between the United States and North Korea?

Margaret got married, Frank was sent back to the states, and Charles made his grand debut. The characters were given more room for development, with many more episodes highlighting individual members of the cast. As the fighting went on, episodes such as "Dreams," and "Follies of the Living— Concerns of the Dead," were constant reminders of the underlying horror and senselessness of war.

DURING ONE EPISODE
(The Later Years)

The 4077th got a new surgeon: Major Charles Emerson Winchester III . . . .

1. Why did Burns leave?

2. What eventually happened to Burns?

3. What was the name of the colonel who transferred Winchester to the 4077th?

4. Winchester won a huge sum of money ($672.17) from a colonel. What game did they play?

5. Who was Winchester's first patient?

6. What was wrong with him?

One of BJ's old friends, who happened to be a chronic practical joker, showed up at the 4077th to enliven things . . . .

7. What was his name?

Hawkeye suggested to Radar that he go to Seoul to get himself a woman and perhaps grow up a bit. Radar never made it, because he was wounded on the way....

8. What was the name of the "bar" Radar was going to visit?

9. What was the title of this episode?

10. What did Hawkeye do to disillusion Radar?

Radar decided that women would go for him if he had a tattoo....

11. What did he choose to have tattooed?

12. Where on his body did he get tattooed?

Sidney Freedman visited the 4077th at a time when everyone was edgy and irritable....

13. What did Winchester do to make Margaret angry?

14. What did Hawkeye do to anger BJ?

15. What was Freedman's prescription for relieving the tension?

16. What song did everyone sing?

If it wasn't one emergency, it was another. A certain lovely nurse invited Hawkeye to spend the weekend with her in Tokyo, but he was unable to get away from the 4077th....

17. Who was that special nurse?

18. Who was going to cover Hawkeye's job for him?

The 4077th got caught up in a mystery novel....

19. What was the title of the book?

20. Who was the author of the book?

*21. How old was the author, and where did she live?

22. How many people were killed in the novel?

23. Where did the murders take place?

24. According to the author, who did it?

It was Lexington and Concord all over again as the 4077th treated some wounded British soldiers....

25. What was the name of the British officer who seemed not to care about his men?

26. A few of the soldiers contracted peritonitis. What caused it?

Father Mulcahy and Corporal Klinger tried to get back penicillin that was stolen from the 4077th....

27. Where was the penicillin hidden?

28. How did Father Mulcahy discover where it was hidden?

Hawkeye struck a superior officer who disgusted him by being able to predict accurately the number of soldiers who would be wounded....

29. What was this officer's rather ironic name?

30. What happened to the charges against Hawkeye?

While the 1952 Summer Olympics were being held, the 4077th held their own Olympics....

*31. Where were the Summer Olympics held?

32. What were the names of the two teams?

33. Who ran the obstacle course for each team?

34. BJ and Hawkeye, the two opposing team captains, had a side bet on the outcome of the M*A*S*H Olympics. What was the prize?

Hawkeye fell in love with a Korean woman....

35. What was her name?

36. For what did she trade her car?

Blue script was going to be exchanged for red script, and Corporal Klinger took the West Point entrance exam....

37. How much did Winchester offer the Koreans for their old script?

38. Why did Klinger want to go to West Point?

Hawkeye and BJ commissioned a local merchant to make a special kind of surgical instrument, and Klinger lost something that belonged to Margaret....

39. What kind of instrument was it?

40. Who made the instrument?

41. Who was the instrument used on first?

42. What did Klinger lose?

It was Hawkeye and BJ vs. Winchester. Hawk and BJ wouldn't bathe until Winchester stopped playing his musical instrument....

43. What was the instrument?

44. In the end, what happened both to Winchester's instrument and to Hawkeye and BJ?

Winchester lent BJ and Hawkeye some money, and then proceeded to ask for favor after favor. Revenge, however, was not too far away as Winchester lost his shirt playing poker....

45. For what did Winchester lend BJ and Hawkeye the money?

46. What did Winchester do when he bluffed?

One of Radar's rabbits was needed for a pregnancy test for Margaret, and a patient held first Winchester and then Klinger hostage....

47. What was the rabbit's name?

48. What was the name of the soldier who took the hostages?

49. Where did he want to go?

50. What had his occupation been prior to the war?

Colonel Potter was all set to retire because someone in the 4077th was sending bad reports about him to ICOR....

*51. Who was the snitch?

52. Why?

Radar's mouse, after taking some of Winchester's pep pills, won a race against a Marine company's mouse....

53. What was the mouse's name?

54. Winchester also took some pep pills, and after doing so wrote an article for a medical journal. What error in syntax did he make?

The 4077th got a new soldier who shot at imaginary gliders, talked to his socks and shoes, and wound up with a Section 8....

55. What was his name?

56. Of what company did he become president after getting his discharge?

Hawkeye and BJ invented a new game. It was a combination of chess, checkers, and various card games, and had absolutely no rules....

*57. What did they call their new game?

Radar helped get the 4077th through a long siege of wounded by playing disc jockey . . . .

58. What song did he play at Colonel Potter's "request" 23 times?

59. Who did the song remind the Colonel of?

There was an exchange of personnel between the 4077th and the 8063rd . . . .

60. Who did the 4077th get?

61. Who did the 8063rd get?

62. What did the surgeon from the 8063rd do to anger Colonel Potter?

Fed up with the slowness of the peace talks, Hawkeye crashed into the talks . . . .

63. Where were the peace talks being held?

64. What was the name of the general Hawkeye pretended to treat?

65. What was wrong with the general?

While BJ was helping out a Korean family, an accident-prone general sought aid at the 4077th . . . .

*66. What was the name of the little girl BJ helped?

*67. BJ was trying to help locate the girl's brother. What was his name?

68. What was the name of the accident-prone general?

69. What accidents did he have?

While Winchester was refusing to talk to anyone because he had been passed over for a promotion back home, Major Freedman was called upon to treat a young, dedicated medic with amnesia . . . .

70. What job was Winchester passed over for?

71. What were Winchester's "last" words?

72. How did Hawkeye and BJ get him to talk again?

73. What did Winchester do in retaliation?

74. What was the name of the soldier with amnesia?

*75. Where was he from?

76. What made him lose his memory?

77. How did Sidney get him to regain his memory?

A nurse who was the same age and who had the same interests as Colonel Potter visited the 4077th....

78. What was her name?

79. What song did the two sing after coming back from the picnic?

In the middle of an unbearable heat wave, Hawkeye and BJ got a bathtub, Radar had his tonsils removed, and Klinger almost got a discharge....

80. From what company did Hawkeye and BJ get the bathtub?

81. To whom did they trade it?

82. What did they get for the tub?

83. How long did Klinger have to wear the sweat suit and mink coat before Colonel Potter would give him the discharge?

When the 4077th ran out of pentothal, Father Mulcahy and Winchester had to deal with the black market....

84. What did the black marketeers steal from Winchester?

North Korea wanted to copy the successful methods of the 4077th, so they sent a spy to work as Winchester's houseboy....

*85. What was the spy's name?

86. The spy came up with the remedy for a mysterious rash. What was the remedy?

While Winchester was instigating a series of practical jokes, Father Mulcahy helped a heroic chopper pilot whose "traveling companion" had been destroyed....

87. What was the name of the chopper pilot?

88. What was the dummy's name?

All the action was viewed through the eyes of a wounded soldier....

*89. What was the soldier's name?

90. What was the only word he said?

Despite protests from BJ, Hawkeye removed a healthy appendix from a colonel who had too high a casualty rate....

91. What was the colonel's last name?

It was Father Mulcahy's turn to write a letter home. In the letter, he told of what it was like to have Christmas in Korea....

92. To whom was the letter written?

93. Father Mulcahy asked Winchester's parents to send him a special Christmas present. What was it?

Hawkeye tried to make time with a beautiful Swedish doctor....

94. What was her name?

95. To help Hawkeye get over the woman, Margaret took him to a movie. What was the title of the movie?

The 4077th had to "bug out" to a cave....

96. What problem did Hawkeye have?

BJ arranged for the families of the 4077th personnel to have a "reunion" party....

*97. What was the date of the party?

 98. At what hotel was it held?

 99. Who did Hawkeye's dad get friendly with?

100. Where was Radar supposed to vacation the first summer after the war ended?

Hawkeye and the others decided to turn Rosie's into their own sovereign nation....

101. What name did they choose for their "country"?

102. What did Hawkeye have for breakfast?

Winchester and Margaret came down with food poisoning....

103. What did they eat that caused it?

During an unusually long siege in OR, each member of the 4077th took a brief nap and had a rather bizarre dream....

104. In Colonel Potter's dream, a young boy was playing in a field. What was the name of the boy?

105. In Hawkeye's dream, his professor asked him to remove his arms. Why?

106. In BJ's dream, what was he wearing?

107. In Margaret's dream, what was she wearing?

108. In Winchester's dream, what was he holding when he started to tap dance?

109. In Father Mulcahy's dream, who was nailed to the cross?

110. In Klinger's dream, what was the name of the restaurant?

Margaret a Communist sympathizer? That's what a Congressman's aide came to investigate . . . .

111. Who was the Congressman?

112. What was his aide's name?

*113. Wally Crighton, a man Margaret dated, founded a supposedly subversive organization. What was its name?

114. What was going to happen to Margaret if she didn't name names?

115. How did Margaret get out of the mess?

116. What was the scandal that the Congressman was later found to have been involved in?

The 4077th tried to keep a woman accused of being a guerilla away from a cold-hearted South Korean officer . . . .

117. What was the officer's name?

Winchester, while drunk, got "married" . . . .

118. What was his bride's name?

119. Who married them?

The 4077th's generator broke down, leaving them without electricity or lights, and Radar received his discharge . . . .

120. What happened to their back-up generator?

121. With no lights, where did they operate at night?

122. How did Klinger get a new generator?

123. Why was Radar being sent home?

124. What happened to his going-away party?

125. What did Radar leave behind in Korea when he went home?

Radar may have left, but he was not forgotten. Klinger found that Radar may have been small, but filling his boots was a big task. And BJ was upset with Radar over an incident back home....

126. What did BJ and Klinger use for a dart board while at Rosie's?

127. Why was BJ angry with Radar?

Father Mulcahy was helping a beautiful nurse study for medical school when she became a little too friendly to suit the Father's tastes....

128. What was her name?

129. What was the nickname given to her by the other nurses?

A clock was superimposed over the screen, counting down in actual time the number of minutes remaining if an operation was to be a success....

130. Roughly, how much time did the surgeons have?

131. What was the patient's name?

132. What was the operation for?

133. What was the name of the donor of the needed part?

134. Who provided the blood for the transfusion?

135. How were they able to buy more time?

The 4077th's new company clerk, Corporal Klinger, wrote a letter home telling his uncle about all that was happening at the 4077th....

136. What was the name of the uncle the letter was written to?

*137. In one part of the letter, Klinger mentioned what Hawkeye thought was the world's funniest joke (the one where the little scrawny guy goes looking for a job at the circus). What was the punch line?

With both Colonel Potter and Major Winchester out of action with the mumps, the 4077th got a new surgeon. He proved to be an excellent surgeon, but unfortunately he cracked under the pressure . . . .

138. What was his name?

139. Where was he from?

140. What medical school had he attended?

*141. He had been stationed at a M•A•S•H unit once before. Where?

142. In coming down with the mumps, what was Winchester's great fear?

143. Who else came down with the mumps?

Margaret wanted a nurse, who had a tendency to cry and get sick in OR, to be transferred . . . .

144. What was the nurse's name?

145. Whose death made Margaret soften her stance toward the nurse?

The 4077th found an abandoned baby of Korean and American parentage who captured all their hearts . . . .

146. Where did the baby eventually end up?

Hawkeye decided to give up drinking because of an unusually large bar tab . . . .

*147. How much did he owe?

148. How long did Hawkeye go without drinking?

While Hawkeye and BJ, as morale officers, put together a beach party, Winchester agonized over his decision to save a soldier's foot rather than his hand. The soldier turned out to be a concert pianist . . . .

149. What was the soldier's name?

150. Where had he gone to college?

*151. What was the title of the Ravel piece that Winchester got the soldier to play?

Colonel Potter was down in the dumps when he got the news that one of his buddies from World War I had died, making the Colonel the only survivor of his group . . . .

*152. What were the names of the four friends from his youth colonel Potter drank a toast to?

153. What was the name of the law firm that kept the brandy?

154. With whom did Colonel Potter share it?

An Asian-American war hero wanted to commit suicide after he was informed that he was being shipped home . . . .

155. What was his name?

156. How did Major Freedman "cure" him?

It was April Fool's Day, with Hawkeye, BJ, Winchester, and Margaret the victims of a classic prank . . . .

157. What were the names of two pranksters?

*158. What did the one colonel like to drink?

A beautiful, famous, female war correspondent fell in love with BJ . . . .

159. What was her name?

The 4077th received 500,000 tongue depressors, and Klinger, to earn some extra money, published a newspaper . . . .

160. Hawkeye constructed a building with the tongue depressors, then blew it up. Why?

161. What was the name of Klinger's paper?

162. Margaret was the paper's beauty editor. What was her column called?

163. What did Winchester write about?

Klinger's goat ate the company payroll, with Hawkeye, as payroll officer, responsible for the money . . . .

*164. How much did the goat eat?

165. What was the name of the officer who investigated the case?

A very sick Klinger was able to talk to a dead soldier . . . .

166. What was the soldier's name?

167. What was the one thing the soldier said he missed the most?

Hawkeye, believing he was near death, made out his will . . . .

168. What did he leave to BJ?

169. Who was to get Hawkeye's Hawaiian shirt?

170. He left Father Mulcahy a nickel. Why?

171. To whom did he will his Groucho Marx disguise?

172. What was Winchester to receive?

173. Who was to get his copy of *The Last of the Mohicans*?

Klinger, of all people, wanted to re-enlist . . . .

174. Why?

175. Which oath did Colonel Potter give him?

It was "Boxing Day" at the 4077th. And for one day, the officers and the enlisted men traded places . . . .

176. Whose custom is "Boxing Day"?

177. With whom did Potter trade jobs?

178. Who became the cook?

179. What were Father Mulcahy's and Hawkeye's jobs?

180. What did BJ and Margaret do?

As the war neared an end, the 4077th buried a time capsule . . . .

181. What was the title of this episode?

182. Who was this episode dedicated to?

183. Whose idea was it to bury the time capsule?

184. Hawkeye said, "Let it represent all of the soldiers who came here as boys and went home as men." What was the object?

185. Who contributed a spark plug?

186. What did Winchester contribute?

187. Father Mulcahy wanted his contribution to be the way "to settle future wars." What was the object?

188. Who contributed a pair of combat boots?

189. What did Klinger contribute?

190. BJ said, "It represents all of the men who didn't make it home." What did he bury?

191. What did Margaret contribute?

192. In addition to the time capsule, what did Margaret and Hawkeye jointly bury?

All good things must come to an end, and with the close of the Korean War, the 4077th was disbanded, and M*A*S*H came to its end.

During The Final Episode

With the war in its waning days, Hawkeye suffered a breakdown and was committed to a mental institution. Meanwhile, back at the 4077th:

—BJ, because of a mix-up, received his orders to go home.

—Klinger, while helping a Korean girl look for her family, fell in love with her.

—Winchester "captured" five Korean musicians.

—Margaret was making her postwar plans with help from her father.

—Father Mulcahy became a certified war hero by rescuing some POWs and, in the process, suffering an injury....

1. What was the title of this episode?

2. What two things did Hawkeye do to force his being committed?

3. What was the underlying cause of Hawkeye's problem?

4. In the opening scene, the members of the 4077th were at a beach party. Where and when was it held?

5. How far did BJ get before the mix-up was discovered?

* 6. What was the name of the surgeon who was supposed to have replaced BJ?

7. What was the name of the Korean girl Klinger helped?

8. What two "distinguishing" characteristics did the girl's father, mother, and brother share?

* 9. What was the title of the musical piece that Winchester tried to teach to the Koreans?

10. Who was the composer?

11. What happened to the musicians?

12. What was Father Mulcahy's injury?

*13. Finally, the war ended. What was the name of the newscaster who brought them the word?

14. The members of the 4077th had one final get-together, during which they talked about their postwar plans. What were Colonel Potter's plans?

15. Nurse Kelly said she was going to work a VA hospital in the States. Where?

16. Rizzo said he had a fool-proof plan on how to get rich. What was it?

17. What were Hawkeye's postwar plans?

18. Igor was going to continue to serve food after the war. To whom?

19. Who was Father Mulcahy going to work with after the war?

20. What did Margaret finally decide to do?

21. For Winchester, life would go pretty much as he expected it would. At what job and at what hospital would he be working?

22. Who interceded on Winchester's behalf to help him get him the job?

23. The biggest surprise of all came from Klinger. What were his plans?

24. What farewell present did Winchester give to Margaret?

25. What memento of Klinger did BJ take with him?

26. How did Hawkeye and BJ say good-bye to Colonel Potter?

27. By what "mode" of transportation did Winchester leave?

28. BJ left on a motorcycle. Where did he get it?

29. What color did he paint it?

30. How did Hawkeye leave?

31. What happened to Sophie?

*32. What were Father Mulcahy's last words?

*33. What were the last words on the show, and who spoke them?

34. What was the one word that BJ couldn't bring himself to say to Hawkeye?

35. How did BJ finally "say" that word?

One of the things that made M*A*S*H such a brilliant success was its cast of characters, each one of whom was unique, yet believable, in his or her own special way. They became living, breathing people with histories all their own.

THE CHARACTERS

HAWKEYE

1. What was his full (first, middle, and last) name?

2. How did he get the nickname "Hawkeye"?

3. Where was he from?

4. What was the name of his home town newspaper?

5. What did he always do to his food before he ate it?

6. What was his dad's name, and what did he do for a living?

7. Was his mom living?

*8. Did he have any brothers or sisters?

*9. In what city did he do his residency?

BJ

10. What does BJ stand for?

11. What was his wife's name?

12. What was his daughter's name?

*13. In what month and year was his daughter born?

14. Who was their babysitter? How old was she when BJ was drafted?

15. What college did BJ go to?

16. What fraternity did he belong to in college?

17. Who was the best man at BJ's wedding?

18. In what city did the Hunnicuts live?

*19. What was their phone number?

20. What was the name of their dog?

*21. How old was BJ when he arrived at the 4077th?

22. Where did he receive his military training?

COLONEL POTTER

23. What was his first name and middle initial?

24. What was his wife's name?

*25. What were her measurements? (Hint: it was also the combination to the company safe.)

*26. When were the Potters married?

*27. Where did the Potters live?

28. What musical instrument did Mrs. Potter play?

29. What was his daughter's name?

30. What were the names of his grandchildren?

31. Who was the Colonel's favorite singer?

32. Who was his favorite author?

33. For what did he receive a Purple Heart during World War II?

34. What branch of the Army was he in before he became a doctor?

35. How many wars had he served in? Name them.

36. What was the name of his horse?

*37. What was the Colonel's religion?

HENRY BLAKE

38. Where was he from?

39. What were the names of his wife?

*40. What were her measurements?

41. Although he had at least four children, the names of only three were ever mentioned. What were their names?

42. What college had he attended?

43. What was his "position" on the college football team?

*44. Who shot out Henry's porch light every year?

FRANK BURNS

45. What was his middle name?

46. What was his nickname?

47. What was his wife's name?

48. In what city did they live?

49. How many cars did he have, and how much was his house worth?

*50. What brand of after-shave did he wear?

51. Where did he receive his military training?

WINCHESTER

52. What was his full (first, middle, and last) name?

53. Where was he from?

*54. What was his home address?

55. What was his sister's name, and what disability did she have?

56. Everyone at the 4077th, except for Winchester, sent handwritten letters home. What did Winchester send?

*57. What famous actress did he once date?

58. What college did he attend, and what year did he graduate?

59. What religion was he?

60. What was the one thing he said he always wanted to be?

RADAR

61. What was his full (first, middle, and last) name?

62. Where did the nickname "Radar" come from?

63. Where was he from?

64. What was his mom's name?

65. What was his uncle's name (the uncle that lives on their farm)?

66. What high school did he attend?

67. What was his dog's name?

68. What was his cow's name?

69. What was his goat's name?

70. What was his favorite drink?

71. What three ranks did he hold while on the show?

*72. What medical treatment was his mom undergoing?

KLINGER

73. What was his first name and middle initial?

74. Where was he from?

*75. What was his home address?

76. What was the name of his favorite baseball team?

77. Quite often he wore the jersey of his favorite baseball team. What was the number on the back?

78. What was the name of his favorite restaurant?

*79. What was its address?

80. What was their specialty?

81. What was Klinger's ethnic background?

82. Who was Gus Nagy?

83. Where did Klinger want his mother to think he was?

84. What was his sister's name?

85. What was his father's nickname?

86. Which of his uncles got out of World War II on a Section 8?

*87. On what date did Klinger start wearing dresses?

88. What two ranks did he hold while on the show?

MARGARET

89. What was her nickname?

90. What was her father's name?

91. What brand of cologne did she wear?

92. What was the inscription on her original wedding ring?

93. What was the inscription on her replacement wedding ring?

94. How long was she engaged?

95. What affectionate nickname did her husband call her?

FATHER MULCAHY

96. What were his first and two middle names?

97. What did his mother and sister call him?

98. What did Colonel Potter usually call him?

*99. To what order did his sister belong?

100. What was her name?

101. What sport did she coach, and where?

102. What musical instrument did she play?

103. What was Father Mulcahy's weight class when he boxed for the Jesuits?

ET AL

104. What was Trapper's full (first, middle, and last) name?

105. What were the names of Trapper's wife and daughters?

106. Trapper once went by a nickname other than Trapper. What was it?

107. Where was Nurse Kelly from?

*108. What was Sparky's real name?

109. Who was Lieutenant Leslie Scorch?

110. Who was the ROK officer who was a semiregular during the first season of M*A*S*H?

111. What was Rizzo's first name?

112. What were the names of Rizzo's wife and son?

113. When he wasn't sleeping, what was Rizzo supposed to be doing?

*114. What was Zale's first name?

*115. What was Zale's wife's name?

116. Where was Zale from?

117. What was Zale's job?

118. What was General Clayton's first name?

119. What was the General's favorite drink?

120. Where was Dr. Borelli from?

*121. What was Igor's last name?

122. Who was Ho-Jon?

123. What was Colonel Flagg's first name?

124. What was Major Freedman's full name?

125. Who was Spearchucker Jones?

126. Who was Ugly John?

127. What was Ginger's last name?

Gertrude Stein said, "A rose is a rose is a rose is a rose." Shakespeare's Hamlet said, "To be or not to be." Douglas MacArthur said, "There is no substitute for victory." Who from M*A*S*H said the following?

QUOTATIONS

1. "Pull down your pants and slide on the ice."

2. "Buffalo bagels!"

*3. "It's a funny thing, war. Never have so many suffered so much so that so few could be so happy."

4. "Jocularity! Jocularity!"

5. "It has been both a privilege and a pleasure and an honor."

6. "Ahhh . . . Bach!"

7. "Nerts to you!"

8. "I can take umbrage, I can take the cake, I can take the A train, I can take two and call me in the morning. But I cannot take this sitting down."

9. "Gentlemen."

10. "Dear Dad . . ."

11. "Ohhh . . . Frank!"

12. "It's nice to be nice to the nice."

13. "It's 3:30! In the blessed a-m!!!"

14. - "I'm sick and tired of you guys always going over my head down to Radar!"

15. "I want my martini so dry . . . I want to see dust on the olive."

16. "May your camel spit nothing but dates."

17. "Courage is something you just can't be afraid to have."

18. "Attention! Attention, all personnel! Incoming wounded! Both shifts report to OR! This is gonna be a long one, folks."

19. "Your permission, sir, to cover up my nakedidity?"

20. "Here's looking up your old address!"

*21. "I'm not sleeping, Radar. I'm inspecting the inside of my eyelids."

22. "Horse hockey-pucks!"

23. "He was the best damn OD we ever had."

24. "Snot! Snot! Snot!"

25. "There it is . . . That's the sound of peace."

M*A*S*H is the perfect example of ensemble TV acting at its best. Each of the performers has proven to be superior performers on the program, and in professional endeavors elsewhere.

THE CAST

Any TRUE M*A*S*H fan should know who portrayed a particular character. Match the actor/actress with the character:

1.	Alan Alda	(a)	Nurse Kelly
2.	Robert Alda	(b)	Captain Sam Pak
3.	Alan Arbus	(c)	General Mitchell
4.	Patrick Adiarte	(d)	Ginger
5.	G. W. Bailey	(e)	Hawkeye
6.	Timothy Brown	(f)	Colonel Flagg
7.	William Christopher	(g)	Spearchucker Jones
8.	Odessa Cleveland	(h)	Major Winchester
9.	Jamie Farr	(i)	Ho-Jon
10.	Mike Farrell	(j)	Dr. Borelli

11.	Johnny Haymer	(k)	General Clayton
12.	Enid Kent	(l)	Henry Blake
13.	Larry Linville	(m)	Rizzo
14.	Jeff Maxwell	(n)	Lieutenant Dish
15.	George Morgan	(o)	BJ Hunnicut
16.	Harry Morgan	(p)	Ugly John
17.	Pat Morita	(q)	Father Mulcahy
18.	Kellye Nakahara	(r)	Trapper
19.	John Orchard	(s)	Hot Lips
20.	Karen Phillip	(t)	Major Freedman
21.	Wayne Rogers	(u)	Colonel Potter
22.	Robert F. Simon	(v)	Sergeant Zale
23.	McLean Stevenson	(w)	Major Burns
24.	David Ogden Stiers	(x)	Klinger
25.	Loretta Swit	(y)	Igor
26.	Herb Voland	(z)	Nurse Bigelow
27.	Edward Winter		

28. Who was the first actor selected for a role on M*A*S*H?

29. Who was the only person in the cast to win an Emmy as an actor, a writer, and a director?

*30. Harry Morgan held a record among the actors on the show. What was it?

31. Which M*A*S*H actor won a Tony award for his role as Sky Masterson in the Broadway play *Guys and Dolls*?

32. What are the names of the three actors who, at various times, portrayed Trapper?

33. What two M*A*S*H actors had minor parts in the movie *With Six You Get Eggroll*?

34. Who was known as "The Bird Man of Malibu" because of his love for birds?

35. Which M*A*S*H actor was a gunnery officer in the Army?

36. Which M*A*S*H actress was once a lead singer for the music group Sergio Mendes and Brazil 66?

*37. What two things did Wayne Rogers and F. Scott Fitzgerald have in common?

38. Which one of the M*A*S*H doctors was actually the son of a doctor?

39. Mike Farrell played the part of a doctor on another TV show, "The Interns." What was his name?

40. What farewell present did the cast give to Gary Burghoff after his final episode?

*41. A M*A*S*H actor attended New Trier High School in Winnetka, Illinois, the same high school that Rock Hudson, Ann Margaret, and Charlton Heston also attended. What was the actor's name?

42. What was Wayne Roger's first TV series after he left M*A*S*H?

43. Which M*A*S*H actor was once a member of the famed comedy group "Second City"?

44. Except for his role on M*A*S*H, Harry Morgan is probably best known for being Sergeant Joe Friday's partner on the TV show "Dragnet." What was his name on that show?

*45. Because he was a pacifist, this M*A*S*H actor refused to fight in World War II and worked instead as a medic. Who was it?

46. Who regularly received letters from women asking for fashion advice?

47. Who played the part of Scott Banning on the soap opera "Days of Our Lives"?

48. Who was the original Charlie Brown in the off-Broadway play *You're a Good Man, Charlie Brown*?

*49. Which M*A*S*H actor played the part of Santini, a mentally retarded student, in the classic movie *The Blackboard Jungle*?

*50. From 1969 to 1971, McLean Stevenson was a regular on "The Doris Day Show." What was his name on the show, and what was his job?

51. Although Alan Alda never played football as a child, he starred in the 1968 movie *Paper Lion*. What part did he play?

52. This M*A*S*H actor has a magical background. He was Doug Henning's co-star as Feldman the Magnificent in the Broadway play *The Magic Show*, and he also appeared in the movie *Magic*. Here's a big hint: think of the "Dreams" episode. Who was it?

*53. Which M*A*S*H actor built gliders in his spare time?

*54. Which M*A*S*H actor held the following positions at Woodward High School: class president for three years; features editor of the school newspaper; president of the Radio Club; manager of the football and basketball teams; star of the varsity tennis team; the Most Outstanding Student; member of the National Honor Society?

55. Which M*A*S*H actor doubled as business manager to Peter Falk and James Caan, among others?

56. In addition to the numerous Emmy nominations he has received for his work on M*A*S*H, Alan Alda was nominated for his portrayal of Caryl Chessman, "The Red Light Bandit." What was the title of this made-for-TV movie?

57. Whose cousin was twice the Democratic Party's nominee for President?

58. Alan Alda was in the movie version of "Same Time Next Year." Who, from M*A*S*H, starred in the 1975 Broadway version?

59. What was McLean Stevenson's first TV series after leaving M*A*S*H?

*60. Who received an Emmy nomination for best "Supporting Actor in a Comedy Series" every year he was on the show?

61. Who was the only cast member to have been stationed in Korea when he was in the Army?

62. On two very popular TV shows, Harry Morgan played Pete Porter, a man who disliked his mother-in-law and who was always complaining about his wife. What were the names of these two shows?

63. Besides M*A*S*H, on what other prime-time series has Wayne Rogers portrayed a doctor?

64. Which member of the M*A*S*H cast had polio as a child?

65. On what TV show has McLean Stevenson been a frequent guest host?

66. What do Gary Burghoff and G. Wood have in common?

67. In 1975, a show created by Alan Alda lasted a whole two months before it was cancelled. What was the name of this short-lived show?

*68. What were their home towns:
Alan Alda? Mike Farrell? Wayne Rogers? Harry Morgan? William Christopher? Jamie Farr? Larry Linville? David Ogden Stiers?

*69. Match the actor with his college:

1. Alan Alda   (a) University of Colorado

2. William Christopher (b) Princeton University

3. Mike Farrell   (c) Juilliard

4. Larry Linville   (d) Wesleyan University

5. Harry Morgan   (e) Fordham College

6. Wayne Rogers   (f) University of Chicago

7. McLean Stevenson   (g) Los Angeles City College

8. David Ogden Stiers   (h) Northwestern University

*70. Match the actor/actress with his or her birth date:

1. Alan Alda   (a) November 4

2. Gary Burghoff   (b) October 31

3. William Christopher (c) April 7

4. Jamie Farr   (d) April 10

5. Mike Farrell   (e) September 29

6. Larry Linville   (f) February 6

7. Harry Morgan   (g) July 1

8. Wayne Rogers   (h) October 20

9. David Ogden Stiers   (i) May 24

10. Loretta Swit   (j) January 28

71. Klinger was a tough guy from Toledo. On what TV series did he play a tough guy from Chicago?

72. Larry Linville played a two-star general at the Pentagon on what TV series?

73. What other medically based comedy series did David Ogden Stiers appear on?

74. On what short-lived TV series did McLean Stevenson play a priest?

*75. On what military-based TV show did Alan Alda have his first major TV featured role?

MASH: THE BOOK

1. Match the person with his hometown:
    1. Father Mulcahy   (a) Boston
    2. Painless   (b) Forrest City, Georgia
    3. Trapper   (c) San Diego
    4. Duke   (d) Hamtramck, Michigan
2. Match the person with his college:
    1. Trapper   (a) University of Nebraska
    2. Hawkeye   (b) University of Georgia
    3. Duke   (c) Dartmouth
    4. Sergeant Vollmer   (d) Androscoggin College
3. How did Trapper acquire his nickname?
4. What was Ezekiel Bradbury Marston V's nickname?
5. How did Spearchucker get his nickname?

6. How did The Swamp get its name?

7. Even the 4077th had a nickname. What was it?

8. Whose middle name was Braymore?

9. What was General Hammond's full name?

10. What was Ugly John's last name?

11. What was Burns's rank?

*12. How old was Hot Lips?

13. What was Hawkeye's marital status?

14. What was Trapper's marital status?

15. What was Hawkeye's dad's name?

16. Who was the 4077th's chief surgeon?

17. What were the "Six o'clock Choppers"?

18. What was Trapper's field of expertise?

19. What was Spearchucker's specialty?

Just as he did in the pilot episode of the TV series M*A*S*H, Hawkeye tried to raise money so that he could send Ho-Jon to his college back in the States. Only the means of raising the money differed. Hawkeye sold photographs of Trapper at a buck apiece....

20. Who did Trapper, when he had a beard, resemble?

21. How much money was raised?

*22. Who was the dean of Hawkeye's college?

Just as in the movie M*A*S*H, the 4077th played a football game against the 325th Evac....

23. Who were the two opposing coaches?

24. What was the 4077th's name for the game?

25. Who were the "ringers" that played for the 325th?

26. Who won the game?

*27. Who scored the winning touchdown?

28. What was the final score?

Hawkeye and Duke arrived at the 4077th together, and they departed together. Both accumulated enough "points" and received their discharges....

29. What farewell presents did Radar and Henry give to them?

30. At what airport did Hawkeye and Duke finally part company?

The sequel to MASH was the rather forgettable *MASH Goes to Maine*. In it, Trapper, Duke, and Spearchucker joined Hawkeye in Maine....

*31. What were the names of Hawkeye's wife and kids?

*32. At what hospital did he do his thoracic residency?

*33. What was the name of the clinic the four of them opened?

*34. Who was Trapper's girlfriend?

A quality TV show such as M*A*S*H attracts quality performers as guest stars, some of whom have gone on to their own successful TV series.

1. He was best known for his role as Lieutenant Howard Hunter on the TV show "Hill Street Blues," but he also appeared as the finance officer in the "Tuttle" episode. What is his name?

*2. Oliver Clark appeared in two episodes, and each time with a different name. The first time he was Tippy Brooks, the crossword-puzzle whiz. Who was he the second time?

3. Val Bisoglio appeared in several episodes as the 4077th's cook. He is best known, however, for being Danny, the owner of Danny's Place, on another TV series. What show was it?

4. The wife of one of the M*A*S*H stars appeared in several episodes playing one of the various nurses. What is her name?

5. This famous actor appeared in one episode as Wendell, an under-age Marine who enlisted in order to impress

his girlfriend back home. He is best known for his roles on the TV shows "Happy Days" and "The Andy Griffith Show." What was his name?

*6. Actress Blythe Danner appeared in one episode. What was her name in the show?

*7. Gary Burghoff appeared once as someone other than Radar. Which character did he play?

8. Tim O'Connor appeared in a few episodes. Once he was Dr. Trager, and another time he was Colonel Spiker. He was also a regular on the TV show "Peyton Place." What was his name on that show?

9. Stuart Margolin appeared in two episodes. In one he was a plastic surgeon who performed a nose job on a soldier, and in the other he was Captain Sherman, a psychiatrist. What was the name of the TV show in which Margolin appeared as con-man Angel Martin?

10. Two of the stars of the TV show "St. Elsewhere" appeared in M*A*S*H. Dr. Westphall played Lieutenant Bricker, the director of a propaganda film, and Dr. Ehrlich played a misassigned gourmet cook. What are the names of these two actors?

11. Former professional football player Alex Karras appeared in one episode as Hawkeye's bodyguard. Alex Karras and Alan Alda worked together one other time. Where?

12. Mrs. Kotter, from the TV series "Welcome Back, Kotter," appeared as Nurse Margie Cutler in several of the early episodes. What is this actress's name?

*13. Who is Joshua Bryant?

14. What do Beeson Carroll and Mike Henry have in common?

15. He appeared in one episode as Colonel Buzz Brighton. He also starred in the movie *Airplane* and played the

part of Dr. Vincent Markham on the TV show "Peyton Place." What is his name?

16. Mariette Hartley appeared in one episode as Inga, a Swedish doctor. She is probably best known for her commercials with James Garner. Who was the sponsor of those commercials?

17. Greg Mullavey appeared in a few episodes. He was also a regular on the TV show "Mary Hartman, Mary Hartman." What was his name on that show?

18. The father and the brother of a M*A*S*H star have appeared on M*A*S*H. The brother appeared only once as a medic, but the father appeared several times as a doctor. What are their names?

19. He was Rocky Balboa's brother-in-law in the three *Rocky* movies. He also appeared on M*A*S*H as the CID man, Lieutenant Willis. What is his name?

20. Gregory Harrison appeared in one episode as Lieutenant Tony Baker. He was best known for his role as Gonzo on what TV series?

*21. Who is Linda Meiklejohn?

22. Officer Baker from the TV show "Chips" appeared in one episode as a GI who asked Radar to look after his Korean wife and their baby. What is the name of this actor?

*23. This veteran character appeared in dozens of episodes usually playing one Korean or another (he was the Korean officer in the "Rainbow Bridge" episode and he was Lieutenant Park in "Guerilla My Dreams"). What is this actor's one four-letter word name?

24. This famous football player (he's a defensive lineman) appeared in one episode as Sergeant Elmo Hitalki, a man who intended to beat up Winchester if the Major did not approve Hitalki's promotion. What is his name?

25. Who played the seemingly straightbacked Colonel Daniel Webster Tucker?

26. Andrew Duggan has appeared in many TV shows, including "12 o'clock High" and "Lancer." On M*A*S*H, he played someone's father. Whose?

27. He played Clifford Ainsley, the manager on "Hot L Baltimore"; David Kane, Ann Romano's boyfriend on "One Day at a Time"; and Digger on one episode of M*A*S*H. Who is he?

28. Robert Ito made several guest appearances on M*A*S*H. He is best known for being Quincy's assistant. What was his name on the TV show "Quincy?"

29. Dennis Dugan appeared in two episodes. In one he was Colonel Potter's son-in-law, and in the other he was a young soldier who wanted to marry a Korean "business girl." On what TV show did Dugan appear as Captain Freedom?

30. On "Mayberry, R.F.D." she was Millie Swanson; on M*A*S*H she was Edwina Ferguson. What is her name?

31. Joan Van Ark played Nurse Erica Johnson on one episode of M*A*S*H. She also was Nurse Annie Carlisle on this early 1970's sitcom. What was the name of this show starring Cleavon Little?

32. Which frequent guest star is a regular on the soap opera "Days of Our Lives?"

33. Pat Morita made several guest appearances in the early years of M*A*S*H. He was best known as being the owner of a hamburger place on the TV series "Happy Days." What was his name on that show?

34. On M*A*S*H she was a famous war correspondent, on "The Name of the Game" she was Peggy Maxwell, and on "McMillian & Wife" she was Sally McMillian. What is her name?

*35. According to the credits in the "Tuttle" episode, who played the part of Tuttle?

36. John Orchard was a regular on M*A*S*H during its first season, playing the part of the "gas passer." He also made a guest appearance a few years later as an Austrailian MP who closed down Rosie's. What was his name that time?

*37. Ned Beatty appeared in one episode as a hard-nosed Division Chaplain. What was the chaplain's name?

38. In one episode, he played Private Carter, a soldier who held Burns hostage in the showers. He is best known, however, for being Jack Tripper on this popular TV comedy show. What is the title of the show?

*39. Catherine Bergstrom appeared in a few episodes as someone's wife. Whose wife?

40. He was a regular on the TV show "The Governor and JJ," "Wendy and Me," and "Convoy." He appeared in one episode of M*A*S*H as a friend of Hawkeye's who was writing a book on the Korean War. What is this actor's name?

41. James Cromwell appeared in one episode as Leo Bardonaro, one of BJ's old friends. He was also a regular on a short-lived TV sitcom in which he played Bill Lewis, a desk clerk at a hotel. What was the name of this show?

42. In one episode of M*A*S*H, Hamilton Camp played the part of Corporal Boots Miller. Camp was also a regular on the TV show "He and She." Who were the two stars of that show?

43. George Lindsey was Captain Roy Dupree when he made a guest appearance on M*A*S*H. What character was George Lindsey synonymous with?

*44. In 1973, a singer had a moderate hit record with a

song called "Dead Skunk." This singer also appeared in a few M*A*S*H episodes as Captain Spaulding. What is his name?

45. On the TV show "Soap" he was Father Timothy Flotsky. And on M*A*S*H, he was the PA announcer. What is his name?

M*A*S*H: THE MOVIE

1. In the movie, Hawkeye was the blond, while Trapper had dark hair. Who played the parts of Hawkeye and Trapper?

2. The other star of the movie was Tom Skerritt. Who did he play?

3. A former professional football player played the part of Spearchucker Jones. What is his name?

4. Sally Kellerman and Jo Ann Pflug were the two most prominent nurses in the movie. Which character did each actress portray?

5. Match the actor with the character he portrayed:

   1. Roger Bowen   (a) Radar

   2. Robert Duvall   (b) Painless

   3. Gary Burghoff   (c) Henry

   4. Rene Auberjonois   (d) Dago Red

5. John Schuck   (e) Burns

6. G. Wood   (f) Ho-Jon

7. Kim Atwood   (g) General Hammond

6. Just about everyone at the 4077th had a nickname. One person had several: "The Pride of Hamtramck," "The Painless Pole," and "Painless." What was his "real" name?

*7. What was Lieutenant Schneider's nickname?

8. What was Father Mulcahy's nickname?

9. Match the nickname with that person's "real" name:

1. Hawkeye   (a) Oliver Harmon Jones

2. Trapper   (b) Benjamin Franklin Pierce

3. Duke   (c) John McIntyre

4. Hot Lips   (d) Augustus Bedford Forrest

5. Radar   (e) Margaret Houlihan

6. Spearchucker   (f) Walter O'Reilly

10. How did Major Houlihan get her nickname?

11. What happened to Major Burns?

12. Painless, the dentist, feared that he was a latent homosexual, and thus wanted to commit suicide. What pill did they give to him?

13. How did they prevent him from committing suicide?

14. Was Hot Lips a real blond?

15. Hawkeye and Trapper were summoned to Tokyo to operate on the son of an American official. What office did this person hold?

16. The 4077th played a big football game for some big bucks. Who was their opponent?

17. How much was the wager?

18. What was the name of the "ringer" the 4077th got to play for them?

19. What pro football team had he once played for?

*20. Who was the quarterback for each team?

21. Who won the game?

*22. What was the final score?

23. What adjective did Sergeant Gorman, the jeep driver played by Bobby Troup, use to describe anything connected to the military?

24. What was unusual about the way the film's final credits were given?

25. What was the last line in the movie?

*26. Who was the only member of the cast to be nominated for an Academy Award for his or her acting performance in the film?

*27. What 1974 movie was an ill-conceived attempt at duplicating the success of M*A*S*H by reteaming Donald Sutherland and Elliott Gould in another irreverent comedy?

ODDS & ENDS is composed of questions which even the most avid M*A*S*H fan might find difficult. It contains extremely pointed questions concerning miscellaneous M*A*S*H facts, as well as background and behind-the-scenes materials derived from many different sources.

ODDS & ENDS

*1. Near what city was the 4077th located? (Spelling counts)

2. What was the 4077th's motto?

3. What was the 8063rd's motto?

4. Who was the "Tokyo Rose" of Korea?

5. What was the name of the dive bar located across the road from the 4077th?

6. What was The Swamp?

7. Where was a patient usually shipped to after being treated at the 4077th?

8. Roughly, what was the 4077th's success rate in treating patients?

*9. According to the home-town mileage sign in the middle of the 4077th's compound, how far was it to San Francisco?

*10. To Burbank?

*11. To Seoul?

*12. To Coney Island?

*13. To Death Valley?

*14. To Decatur?

*15. To Honolulu?

*16. To Toledo?

17. What was the title of the M*A*S*H theme song?

18. Who wrote it?

19. Match the date with the event in M*A*S*H history:

1. 17 September 1972   (a) Henry dies

2. 8 October 1974   (b) The last episode is filmed

3. 18 March 1975   (c) The first episode to be
                        filmed entirely without a
4. 14 January 1983   laugh track

                        (d) M*A*S*H debuts

20. What was M*A*S*H's original time slot (day and hour)?

*21. What magazine, a few weeks after M*A*S*H's debut, said the following: "M*A*S*H, which began as one of the most promising series of the new season, is now one of the biggest disappointments....It is as bleached-out as 'Hogan's Heroes.' "?

22. Who was the original producer of M*A*S*H?

*23. He left M*A*S*H to produce what show?

24. What company produced M*A*S*H?

*25. What studio was used for filming M*A*S*H?

*26. Where were the on-location shots filmed?

*27. Who was the show's medical advisor?

*28. After its first season on the air, where in the ratings did M*A*S*H finish?

29. What actor, who starred in several TV series, including "Hennessey," "Mobile One," and "The People's Choice," directed dozens of the early M*A*S*H episodes?

*30. Glen Charles and Les Charles wrote the episode entitled "The Late Captain Pierce." What popular NBC sitcom did they later produce?

31. Mary Kay Place co-wrote several M*A*S*H episodes. On what TV show was she Loretta Haggers?

*32. What was the episode in which Alan Alda made his debut as director?

*33. "The Novocaine Mutiny," the episode in which Hawkeye was put on trial for mutiny, marked whose M*A*S*H directorial debut?

*34. What was the only episode (it was a two-parter) that had two directors?

*35. The first episode that Mike Farrell directed was the one in which Winchester fell for a Korean "business girl." What was the title of this episode?

*36. In what episode did Klinger make his debut?

37. What was the only improvised episode?

38. In addition to a character who dressed in drag, what did the TV show M*A*S*H and the movie *Tootsie* have in common?

39. According to Jamie Farr, what were the three favorite dresses he wore as Klinger?

40. Jamie Farr's favorite M*A*S*H episode was the one in which he dressed up as the Statue of Liberty. What was that episode's title?

41. Which episode was Loretta Swit's favorite?

42. Whose favorite was "The Army-Navy Game"?

43. Larry Linville's favorite was one that broke ground for M*A*S*H. For the first time, in this episode a good guy, a friend, died. Which episode was it?

44. Whose favorite was "The Interview"?

45. William Christopher's favorite was one in which he, as Father Mulcahy, was the central character. Which one was it?

46. Which episode was David Ogden Stier's favorite?

*47. Alan Alda couldn't confine himself to selecting just one favorite; in an article in TV Guide, he listed 23! Name any five.

*48. What was the title of the last episode to have actually been filmed?

49. Who sent the following telegram to the cast: "I'm relieved to hear that peace is at hand."?

50. Who congratulated the cast by saying, "I hoped this war would never end."?

51. How much did CBS charge for one thirty-second commercial during the final episode?

52. The final episode was far and away the most-watched program in TV history. What show previously had had that distinction?

53. Who were the only two cast members to have been with the show during its entire ten-plus year run?

*54. In all how many M*A*S*H episodes were there?

55. True or false: The set of M*A*S*H has been sent to the Smithsonian Institute?

56. M*A*S*H was the only comedy show to win this prestigious award. What award?

57. What was the title of the PBS documentary done on M*A*S*H?

*58. Which Chicago TV station produced it?

59. Who was the narrator?

60. A M*A*S*H spin-off series is scheduled to air, beginning in the fall of 1983. What is the title?

61. Who is going to star in the show?

62. The TV series M*A*S*H was based on the movie *M*A*S*H*. Who directed the movie?

*63. Who wrote the screen play?

64. How many Academy Award nominations did *M*A*S*H* receive?

*65. Who walked away with the movie's only Oscar?

66. There have been only a few successful movies done on the Korean War. *M*A*S*H* and *The Bridges at Toko-Ri* are two of them. What other one starred Gregory Peck?

*67. A person connected with the TV M*A*S*H had a minor role in *The Bridges at Toko-Ri*. Who was it?

68. Both the TV series and the movie *M*A*S*H* have something that the original book does not. What is it?

69. Who wrote the original book?

*70. What is the author's real name?

71. How does W. C. Heinz figure in the writing of the book?

*72. What M.A.S.H. unit did the author serve with when he was in Korea?

73. What was Sidney Freedman's definition of "meatball surgery"?

*74. What was "Hoops" Potter's 4077th record?

75. What type of shirt did Hawkeye wear during the opening credits of each show?

Now that you know all there is to know about M*A*S*H it is time to test your total recall. Here are 25 questions on things that occurred at various places throughout the book. Score yourself as follows (four points for each correct answer):

100–92: a Surgeon General 91–84: a Masterful Medic
83–76: a Competent Corpman 75–68: a Buck Private
Under 68: Candidate for a Section 8

THE M*A*S*H EXAM

1. What medical school had Captain Jonathan Tuttle attended?

2. What were the names of Henry's wife?

3. When Harry Morgan appeared as General Bartford Hamilton Steele, what song did he sing at Hawkeye's court martial?

4. What did Klinger dress as when General MacArthur visited the 4077th?

5. When Radar was promoted to Second Lieutenant, what reason for the promotion did Sergeant Woodruff give to Colonel Potter?

6. Actor Oliver Clark appeared in two episodes of M*A*S*H. The first time he was Tippy Brooks, the crossword-puzzle whiz. What part did he play the second time?

7. From what school did Radar take a correspondence course in creative writing?

8. Roughly, what was the 4077th's success in treatment rate?

9. What was Hawkeye's boot size?

10. "It's a funny thing, war. Never have so many suffered so much so that so few could be so happy." Who said that line?

11. What is a five-letter Yiddish word for bedbug?

12. Karen Phillip, aka Lieutenant Dish, was the lead singer for what 1960s group?

13. In the "Point of View" episode, what was the only word that Private Rich, the patient, said?

14. What was the name of Klinger's favorite baseball team?

15. What was the name of the famous, beautiful, female war correspondent who fell in love with BJ?

16. Gary Burghoff once appeared as someone other than Radar. Who did he appear as?

17. In the "Dear Sigmund" episode, what did Winchester do to anger Margaret?

18. Trapper once had a nickname other than Trapper. What was it?

19. Which one of the cast members had a cousin who was twice the Democratic Party's nominee for President?

20. What is "triage"?

21. What is the title of the Mozart piece Winchester was teaching to the five North Korean musicians in the final episode?

22. Who wrote *The Rooster Crowed at Midnight*?

23. After Burns passed out from drinking too much, Hawkeye and BJ put a toe-tag on him. What did it say?

24. He is best known for being Lieutenant Howard Hunter

on the TV show "Hill Street Blues," but he also appeared as the finance officer in the "Tuttle" episode. What is his name?

25. What were the final words of the final episode, and who said them?

THE ANSWERS

DURING ONE EPISODE
(The Early Years)

1. A three-day pass in Tokyo with Lieutenant Maggie Dish.

2. Father John Mulcahy.

3. Lieutenant Dish.

4. So that he could go to college at Hawkeye's alma mater.

5. Charlie Lee.

6. Henry's 100-year-old oak desk.

7. Young Hee.

8. He won her in a "fixed" poker game.

9. Sergeant Baker.

10. The frame from the picture of his mother.

11. Her ivory-handled hair brush.

12. Ho-Jon

13. After gathering everyone together, Hawkeye said that
    he had placed a special dye on some of the stolen
    objects and that the guilty person's fingernails would
    turn blue. In fact, he had not placed any dye on the
    objects, but Ho-Jon incriminated himself by hiding
    his hands.

14. General Barker.

15. Give him a high colonic and send him on a long
    march with full pack.

16. Lieutenant Margie Cutler.

17. Sergant Flacker: his nickname was "Killer."

18. 3099th.

19. 97 wins, zero loses, and three arrests.

20. "Cowboy"; John Hodges.

21. Jean Hodges, Box 743, Reno, Nevada.

22. He was shot at on the golf course, a jeep crashed
    through his tent, his chair blew up, and the latrine
    blew up with Henry inside.

23. Lieutenant Bricker.

24. General Clayton.

25. "Yankee Doodle Doctor."

26. Major Burns.

27. The introduction (with General Clayton) and the clos-
    ing (with Hawkeye) were to be saved; everything else
    was to be destroyed, except for one copy for General
    Clayton.

28. Edwina Ferguson.

29. The nurses, led by Lieutenant Cutler, were refusing to

go out with the guys until someone went out with Edwina.

30. Linda Sue.

31. Elroy Fimple.

32. Holtzman's Department Store.

33. Lieutenant Louise Anderson.

34. Sister Theresa's.

35. Jonathan Tuttle.

36. When Hawkeye was a kid and got into trouble, he blamed it on his imaginary friend, Jonathan Tuttle.

37. Battle Creek, Michigan.

38. 1924.

39. 6'4"; 195 lb.; auburn; hazel.

40. Druid, reformed.

41. Harry and Frieda (which were also the names of Larry Gelbart's parents).

42. Berlinisha Polytechnisho.

43. Fourteen.

44. He jumped out of a helicopter without a parachute.

45. Major Murdoch, a tall, skinny guy.

46. "Buzz" Brighton.

47. He banged his ring constantly.

48. Next to the PA speaker.

49. Milk.

50. The Triple A Diploma Company of Delavan, Indiana.

51. 3268 (he added the two numbers up).

52. Yes.

53. Henry.

54. Tommy Gillis.

55. *You Never Hear the Bullet*.

56. No. The author heard the bullet that claimed his life.

57. He lost them in a poker game.

58. He traded them to the cook for a leg of lamb with mint jelly.

59. He stole them from Hot Lips.

60. "A baby's bottom."

61. Because Henry was going to make them pull double shifts until replacements were found.

62. Hawkeye and Trapper convinced Burns that the area was loaded with gold. Burns, being a greedy person, asked that the transfers be torn up.

63. Private Thompson.

64. A shell fragment was stuck behind the colon. It was in a spot that even Burns admitted anyone could have missed.

65. The CIA's.

66. Hawkeye's and Trapper's.

67. AFS 72485, plus three circles and a square.

68. Hundreds of propaganda leaflets went flying. They read (and were, oddly enough, in English): "Give yourselves up. You can't win. Douglas MacArthur."

69. Navy defeated Army 42 to 36.

70. All he needed, he said, was one rich kid with bad tonsils.

71. "Dear Radar, This is the best restaurant I ever ate in. Good luck, Hawkeye."

72. 7 lb. 2 oz.; 21 inches.

73. Joey Foreman.

74. Lieutenant Erica Johnson.

75. "Bung chow." It means, "Your daughter's pregnancy brings much joy and happiness to our village."

76. Captain Hildebrand.

77. 5 o'clock Charlie.

78. Six weeks.

79. Father Mulcahy.

80. Burns had wanted 5 o'clock Charlie to be shot down all along. General Clayton finally gave in after Charlie mistakenly bombed his jeep.

81. Tai Dong, which was about seven miles south of the 4077th.

82. Major Stoner, Adjutant Inspector General; COM-SERVPAC in Honolulu.

83. Because Baxter was under indictment for influence peddling.

84. A soft-ice-cream maker.

85. The 4077th's latrine.

86. Corporal Phil Walker.

87. Lieutenant Willis.

88. They blackmailed him. After Willis got drunk, Hawkeye and Trapper, with help from Radar, convinced him that he had been fooling around with some nurses, and that they had pictures to prove it.

89. Kim.

90. A nearby mine field.

91. O'Brian.

92. Majors Burns and Houlihan.

93. A gurney race.

94. Wing-tip shoes.

95. Nurse Meg Cratty, who brought with her a pregnant woman as an example of the fine work done by Henry Blake.

96. Sergeant Condon.

97. She was Succotash Queen at Illinois Normal when they met at a Freshman Mixer. Henry then begged her to go out with him.

98. Milt Jaffe; he's a gynecologist.

99. After going through normal military channels, Hawkeye and Trapper struck out. They then went to Radar, who traded Henry's grill for an incubator.

100. General MacArthur's headquarters.

101. A chopper came and fired several machine-gun rounds into the bushes where he was hiding.

102. "Whiplash Wang."

103. It made a thump.

104. $50.

105. General Mitchell.

106. Gary.

107. Three days and three nights in Tokyo and the Officers' Club..

108. Officers would be allowed to have their "families" use the facilities as well, at which point Hawkeye proceeded

to more or less adopt everyone in the camp as his family.

109. Nancy Sue Parker.

110. Independence, Ohio.

111. Twenty-three years old.

112. Ohio State, where she was a cheerleader.

113. She gave him a "tonsillectomy" (i.e., a passionate kiss).

114. Futterman; he was in love with Tokyo and wanted a pass to spend some time there.

115. The cake was for Burns; it came from Radar.

116. Murphy; she wanted a hair dryer.

117. Before Klinger would part with his hair dryer, he wanted a Section 8. Hawkeye and Trapper signed, but Burns wouldn't.

118. His golf bag.

119. 10½ C.

120. Private Weston.

121. They blackmailed Burns. Hawkeye and Trapper tricked him into admitting that he had paid $400 for a copy of his med school finals..

122. Pioneer Aviation.

123. Rainbow Bridge.

124. Dr. Lin Tam.

125. University of Illinois.

126. Laverne Esposito.

127. Father Mulcahy.

128. A white wedding gown.

129. "Iron Guts" Kelly.

130. Colonel Wortman.

131. Rub the pearls across your teeth. If they feel smooth, then they're fake.

132. He swiped Hawkeye's watch.

133. Hawkeye took it from Trapper and gave it to the finance officer. As payroll officer, Hawkeye was about $3,000 short, and Trapper's winnings covered the loss.

134. Kim Luck.

135. General Bartford Hamilton Steele.

136. "Mississippi Mud."

137. He was promoted to three-star general and transferred to the Pentagon.

138. The 44th EVAC.

139. It was 5 o'clock Charlie! He dropped propaganda leaflets.

140. A Greek outfit attached to the UN forces.

141. Private Charles Lamb.

142. A hardship discharge. (Henry: "A death in the family?" Radar: "Almost.")

143. Hawkeye made a Spam lamb.

144. He had an ulcer.

145. The Army was no longer giving discharges for ulcers.

146. The Statue of Liberty.

147. Leviticus 10:9. ("Drink no wine nor strong drink...")

148. He was so unaccustomed to speaking in front of a large group that to calm his nerves he drank a little too much wine.

149. Burns, Trapper said, slipped on a bar of soap.

150. A razor, toothpaste, a bar of soap, six aspirin, a washcloth, and four Oreo cookies.

151. Colonel Reese.

152. Liver and fish. ("I've eaten a river of liver and an ocean of fish.")

153. Adam's Ribs in Chicago.

154. Dearborn 5-7500.

155. Dearborn 5-2750.

156. Mildred Feeney.

157. He said they needed the ribs to practice on, since they weren't allowed to practice on the real thing. And they needed the sauce to use as blood.

158. Sergeant Tarola.

159. Joliet, Illinois.

160. Cole slaw.

161. Dr. Borelli.

162. An arterial transplant in the patient's leg.

163. Sergeant Schwartz.

164. A teacher, a lawyer, a priest, and an engineer.

165. A chaplain.

166. Danny MacShane.

167. Soong Hee.

168. She had tuberculosis.

169. Radar Benjamin Franklin John Henry Kwan.

170. He drew the short sausage.

171. Klinger was "Grumpy," and Radar was "Snow White".

172. "Abyssinia, Henry."

173. A pin-stripe suit.

174. Hawkeye; they hugged each other.

175. "You behave yourself, or I'm gonna come back and kick your butt." Radar.

176. His plane was shot down over the Sea of Japan.

177. Radar, in the OR.

TERMINOLOGY

1. Mobile Army Surgical Hospital.

2. Operating Room.

3. Office of the Day.

4. The sorting of and allocation of treatment for the wounded according to a system of priorities designed to maximize the number of survivors.

5. The large artery located near the heart. The branches from the aorta carry blood to the different parts of the body.

6. A toilet.

7. The forced moving of a unit to a new location caused by a possible invasion from the enemy or other life-threatening situation.

8. An instrument used to control or stop the flow of blood from a vein or artery.

9. At once.

10. Local Indigenous Personnel.

11. A South Korean term for a slave or servant derived from the Japanese word *musame*, which is the generic word for woman.

12. An acute illness characterized by impaired renal function. There is usually nausea, vomiting, fever, and chills. It is believed to be caused by a virus; it occurs in Europe and Asia; and there is no specific treatment for it.

13. A type of suture made from sheep's intestines.

14. Another type of suture. The "3-0" refers to the thickness of the silk in millimeters.

15. The section of the military codes that allows for discharge from the service because of a mental or psychological problem.

16. The manual compression of a stopped heart in the hope that the heart will again start beating.

17. A general anesthetic commonly used in surgery.

18. A pad of gauze or cotton used to absorb excess blood.

19. The ballooning out of a blood vessel.

20. Pertaining to the chest.

21. An apparatus used to grow bacteria in order to study them.

22. The colloquial name given to surgery done at M.A.S.H units. The primary object was to save the patient; the fine tuning was to be done elsewhere.

23. The cutting away of the damaged sections of bowel, or intestines, and sewing the undamaged sections together.

24. Infection of the abdominal lining following a wound to the stomach.

25. Used in general surgery or in dissecting.

26. A drug used to reduce swelling and inflammation.

27. The washing of a wound with water or saline solution to kill bacteria.

28. A hormone secreted by the adrenal glands commonly used to revive a cardiac arrest patient.

29. The state of having a body temperature that is lower than normal. It is sometimes brought about intentionally to slow the bodily reactions during surgery.

30. A "gas passer," or one who administers anesthesia.

During One Episode
(The Middle Years)

1. Trapper had Radar give Hawkeye a kiss.

2. Kimpo.

3. "How's it goin', ferret face?"

4. 1600 hours on 19 September 1952.

5. He gave him a horse he had found; Potter named her Sophie.

6. They gave him a carved wooden bust of the Colonel (although it looked more like the artist, Mr. Shin, than it did Potter)..

7. "Digger" Detmuller.

8. As a security precaution in connection with Eisenhower's visit to Korea, neither phone calls nor telegrams were allowed to be sent..

9. His allowance.

"Smilin' Jack" Mitchell.

Club soda.

2. He had the uncanny ability to launch a hypodermic needle with a spoon and have the needle land point down in an orange.

13. 843.

14. "Dangerous Dan."

15. Sixteen.

16. Colonel Maurice Hollister.

17. Attila the Hun.

18. Private Davis.

19. He ran a pony ride at Palisades Park in New Jersey.

20. Griswold.

21. He let the 4077th borrow a tank to scare off a sniper.

22. Lieutenant Chivers.

23. An ingrown toenail.

24. Two bottles of eight-year-old scotch.

25. Meg Cratty.

26. "Mama san."

27. The story of Androcles and the Lion.

28. He read the kids the portion of the Army Manual on how to clean and dismantle a rifle.

29. He received a shell fragment in the eye—an egg-shell fragment.

30. He said there were five stars above, and they were directly beneath the brightest star.

31. Collette, whom he met in a hospital during World War II.

32. Helen Rapapport.

33. "Should Father Coughlin Be President?"

34. Captain Arnold T. Chandler.

35. Idaho.

36. In Colorado.

37. Fifty-seven.

38. His clothes.

39. Hemorraghic fever.

40. Radar, Klinger, Igor, and Zale.

41. Six days R 'n' R in Tokyo.

42. Tugarraf. (Farragut spelled backwards; he cheated.)

43. Radar.

44. Because his mother doesn't read too fast.

45. He was shot by a sniper.

46. In the rear end.

47. He had nail polish on his toes.

48. Chaffee.

49. It was a chrome Colt 45, made in 1884, with a bone grip handle.

50. Major Burns.

51. He's a dentist.

52. Jeannine.

53. Sheri Pershing Potter.

54. 8½ lbs.

55. He would order the tomato juice only for a pair of nylons, which he gave to Hot Lips. He got the nylons from Klinger in exchange for a two-day pass in Seoul.

56. He turned it down; he's allergic to it.

57. 1680.

58. Sol and Sols.

59. Dr. Samuel Sax.

60. He gave the father some tobacco; he gave the mother a vegetable grater; he gave the pregnant woman his name and told her where he could be reached, so that he could deliver her baby; and he gave the young girl a few comic books and some candy bars.

61. Nurse Abel.

62. Coner.

63. He had a chopper pick it up and drop it on the Colonel.

64. "Emotionally exhausted and morally bankrupt."

65. At an aid station at the front (still sleeping).

66. 11 October 1952.

67. Colonel Carmichael.

68. $300; in Radar's teddy bear.

69. Burns wasn't doing his job, triage, properly. Hawkeye told him to go back and do it right. Burns then hit his head on the door.

70. Caryle Walton Breslin.

71. Doug; he was in the Navy at the time, but his career was in advertising.

72. Clete Roberts.

73. Father Mulcahy said he was especially moved when, on a cold day, he saw the surgeons trying to warm their hands from the steam that rose from an open wound.

74. The food was green, except for the vegetables, of

course, and the blood wasn't green—it was always red.

75. It was filmed in black and white.

76. Lieutenant Colonel Donald Penobscott.

77. 203 in a class of 600.

78. A Korean family and their ox.

79. Toby Wilder and Dickie Barber.

80. Clarence Vanderhaven.

81. Hermitage Hill.

82. "Stinky."

83. Basketball.

84. Sergeant Woodruff.

85. To settle a poker debt that Woodruff owed Hawkeye and BJ.

86. "Efficiency, punctuality, and bugling above and beyond the call of duty."

87. Major James Oberman.

88. Indians 5; Yankees 4.

89. Yankees 8; Indians 1.

90. Sergeant Callan.

91. It was to help pay for his wife's operation.

92. Major General Ted Korshak.

93. Lieutenant Baker.

94. Lieutenant Tony Baker.

95. Dear Sigmund.

96. BJ.

97. BJ filled Burns's foxhole with water and then had Sidney yell, "Air raid!" Burns jumped in, face first.

98. Jerry O'Donnell.

99. Radar wrote it on behalf of Colonel Potter.

100. Floyd Hayden.

101. Kwa Paw, Oklahoma.

102. She had colic.

103. They had to clean out her insides.

104. Chou Won Ho.

105. Syn Paik.

106. University of Chicago, class of '49.

107. Danny Fitzsimmons.

108. Boom Boom Gallagher.

109. With Hawkeye giving him directions on the radio, Father Mulcahy performed a tracheotomy on a soldier in a jeep in the middle of a battle.

110. Sergeant Billy Tyler.

111. Running back.

112. Iowa.

113. He had his leg amputated.

114. He wanted to commit suicide.

115. By going for the "short pass" and continuing to try.

116. Colonel Harold Becket.

117. Five days.

118. Buying food for the troops.

119. Cho Lin.

120. Soony.

121. Riding a white pony.

122. It's a silent ceremony; no words are spoken.

123. Famous Las Vegas Writers' School.

124. When Burns was a kid, one of his neighbors was a sickly child. This child once was riding on a sled when he lost control of it and crashed into a car.

125. They argued with each other for a full day.

126. In arguing with Hawkeye, BJ said one thing he hated about Hawkeye was that he always had to get in the last word. When Hawkeye and BJ made up, Hawkeye agreed to let BJ, for once, get in the last word. BJ said, "Thank you." To which Hawkeye replied, "You're welcome."

127. Magic.

128. Lieutenant Willie Sutton.

129. 94 hours and 19 minutes.

130. Colonel Potter.

131. Major Burns.

132. From Klinger.

133. A body cast.

134. Vantz.

135. 38 across.

136. *The New York Times*.

137. Tippy Brooks.

138. Aboard the U.S.S. *Essex*.

139. Lieutenant Carrie Donovan, a nurse.

140. She had received a "Dear Jane" letter from her husband.

141. Vern Parsons.

142. *My Darling Clementine*.

143. "Horses, cowboys, and horses."

144. Jack Benny and John Wayne.

145. They worked on patients during the day and nurses through the night.

146. Father Mulcahy.

The Korean War

1. At 4 a.m. (Korean time) on 25 June 1950.

2. Harry S Truman.

3. Syngman Rhee.

4. South Korea, United States, Great Britain, Canada, Turkey, Thailand, the Philippines, New Zealand, Australia, France, Greece, the Netherlands, Colombia, Belgium, Ethiopia, Luxembourg, and South Africa. In addition, Denmark, India, Norway, Sweden, and Italy supplied medical units, but did not fight.

5. Inchon.

6. Yalu River.

7. The United States did not want to get into a war with China and quite possibly World War III.

8. General Omar Bradley.

9. President Truman fired General MacArthur.

10. General Matthew B. Ridgway.

11. It was the code name for a UN counteroffensive that began 7 March 1951. Its primary objective was to wipe out the North Korean army; its secondary objective was to capture land, especially to force the Communists out of Seoul.

12. It was the code name for an exchange of prisoners that took place at Panmunjom in January 1953. About 6000 Communists were exchanged for a like number of UN prisoners.

13. 27 July 1953 at 10 p.m. Korean time.

14. The 38th parallel.

15. Dwight D. Eisenhower.

16. Democratic People's Republic (North Korea) and Republic of Korea (South Korea).

17. Pyonggang (North Korea) and Seoul (South Korea).

18. A "police action."

19. 54,246 dead and 103,284 wounded.

20. North Korea captured the United States ship the U.S.S. *Pueblo*, and held it and its crew members captive for about a year.

DURING ONE EPISODE
(The Later Years)

1. He was so upset over Margaret's marriage that he went berserk while on leave in Tokyo.

2. He was promoted to Lieutenant Colonel and transferred to a VA hospital in Indiana.

3. Horace Baldwin.

4. Cribbage.

5. Dr. Berman.

6. He had an aneurysm near his heart.

7. Leo Bardonaro.

8. The Pink Pagoda.

9. "Fallen Idol."

10. After drinking too much the night before, Hawkeye got sick in OR and had to leave a patient. Later,

Hawkeye made matters even worse when he told Radar off.

11. A teddy bear.

12. His tush.

13. He touched his nose and wouldn't admit it.

14. Hawkeye, after smelling each piece of food, would tell Bj what disgusting smell it reminded him of. BJ was then unable to eat.

15. A giant bonfire.

16. "Keep the Home Fires Burnin'."

17. Nancy Gilmore.

18. Winchester.

19. *The Rooster Crowed at Midnight*.

20. Abigail Porterfield.

21. 97; Sydney, Australia.

22. Eleven.

23. Huntly Manor.

24. Avery Updike.

25. Major Ross.

26. The drinking of tea with an abdominal wound.

27. Underneath a bell near an abandoned school.

28. A soldier told him about it in a confessional.

29. Victor Bloodworth.

30. After Hawkeye operated on him and saved his life, Bloodworth agreed to drop the charges.

31. Helsinki.

32. Yellow Blackbirds and Pink Elephants.

33. Sergeant Ames for Hawk's team, and Penobscott, for BJ's team. Ames, who was overweight and out of shape, beat Penobscott.

34. BJ, the loser, had to push Hawkeye around in a wheel-chair for a month.

35. Kyong Soon.

36. An ox.

37. Ten cents on the dollar.

38. To get out of the Army. He'd simply cheat on the first exam, get thrown out, and go back home.

39. A vascular clamp.

40. Mr. Shin.

41. Private Cohen.

42. Margaret's wedding ring.

43. A french horn.

44. Margaret ran over Winchester's french horn with a jeep. And everyone washed BJ and Hawkeye by hosing them down.

45. BJ needed money for a down payment on a piece of land he and Peg wanted to buy. Hawkeye needed money to pay his bar tab.

46. He whistled loudly.

47. Fluffy.

48. Lieutenant Tom Martinson.

49. Back home to Ohio.

50. He was an Associate Professor of Art History (Yale, class of '48).

51. Corporal Joe Benson.

52. He was sent there as a spy when ICOR received a complaint from a general who didn't like the way he was treated at the 4077th.

53. Daisy.

54. The entire article consisted of one very long sentence.

55. Corporal "Boots" Miller.

56. Novelty Toy Co.

57. "Double Cranko."

58. "Sentimental Journey."

59. Doris Day.

60. Captain Roy Dupree (University of Arkansas, class of '44) and Lorraine Anderson, an old friend of Margaret's.

61. Hawkeye and Nurse Bigelow.

62. BJ and Winchester tricked Dupree into taking Sophie for a midnight ride around the compound.

63. Panmunjom.

64. Tomlinson.

65. Gastritis.

66. Kim Sing.

67. Chou Duc Sing.

68. Marion Prescott.

69. He broke his ankle, sprained his wrist, and was stung by one of Radar's bees.

70. Chief of Thoracic Surgery at Massachusetts General Hospital.

71. "Never, never, never!"

72. They sent him a phony telegram which said that they

(the hospital board) had reconsidered their earlier decision and were now considering him for the job.

73. He capsized the tent on BJ and Hawkeye.

74. Sergeant Jerry Nielson.

75. Hartford, Connecticut.

76. He was asked by his mom to look after his younger brother, Stevie, who was also in Korea. He then found Stevie dead in a bunker on Hill 403.

77. Sidney hypnotized him, then, with help from BJ and Hawkeye, re-enacted what happened on Hill 403 that day.

78. Lil Rayburn.

79. "Harrigan."

80. Abercrombie and Fitch.

81. Sergeant Rhoden.

82. Scotch and a gallon of strawberry ice cream for Radar.

83. Twenty-four hours. (He only had one hour to go when he gave up.)

84. His polar suit.

85. Kyong.

86. Apply boiled bark to the rash.

87. Captain Toby Hill.

88. "Little Mac."

89. Private Hank Rich.

90. "Thanks."

91. Lacey.

92. His sister.

93. His old toboggan cap.

94. Inga Halverson.

95. *Casablanca*.

96. He suffered from claustrophobia.

97. The weekend of March 28th.

98. Hotel Pierre in New York City.

99. Mrs. Potter.

100. At "the Cape of Cod" (the Winchesters invited Radar and his family to spend the summer there).

101. Rosieland.

102. Cereal and beer.

103. Spoiled pheasant.

104. Potter.

105. Because he had fallen asleep in class and was unable to tell the professor the procedure for reattaching a limb.

106. A tux.

107. A wedding gown.

108. Sparklers.

109. A wounded, bleeding soldier.

110. Tony Packo's Cafe.

111. Daniel Lurie.

112. Williamson.

113. Freedom For Tomorrow

114. She would be subpoenaed and would have to testify before "the committee" (probably HUAC).

115. Hawkeye, BJ, and Winchester dropped some hints about Margaret's romantic past. Williamson then made

a pass at her, and Klinger, hiding in her closet, caught it all on film. They threatened to send the pictures to Williamson's wife.

116. Lurie was having an affair with Williamson's wife.

117. Lieutenant Park.

118. Donna Marie Parker.

119. A bartender.

120. It was stolen.

121. They operated outside by the headlights of jeeps and trucks.

122. He was going to give a case of scotch to Sergeant Hondo McKee for a generator, but when that deal fell through, he stole the generator from General Van Kirk.

123. He received a DA-7 hardship discharge when his uncle Ed passed away.

124. It had to be cancelled when the 4077th received incoming wounded.

125. His teddy bear.

126. A hand-drawn picture of Radar.

127. BJ's wife and daughter met Radar at the airport in San Francisco. His daughter mistook Radar for him.

128. Lieutenant Gail Harris.

129. "Nurse-Doctor."

130. Twenty minutes.

131. George.

132. A lacerated aorta.

133. Harold.

134. Winchester.

135. Hawkeye packed the wound with ice, thus intentionally bringing on hypothermia and slowing down his vital signs.

136. Abdul.

137. "Is that all you do . . . bird imitations?"

138. Captain Stephen J. Newsome.

139. Chicago.

140. Johns Hopkins.

141. In the Pusan Perimeter.

142. That the mumps would leave him permanently sterile.

143. Klinger.

144. Lieutenant Sandra Cooper.

145. A stray dog she had grown fond of.

146. At a nearby monastery.

147. $38.20.

148. One week.

149. Private David Jordan.

150. Juilliard.

151. "Concerto for the Left Hand." (The Austrian pianist, Paul Wittgenstein, lost his right hand while serving in World War I. He asked Ravel to write a piece for the left hand only.)

152. Stein, Grusky, Ryan, and Gianelli.

153. Smith, Smith, and Brown.

154. Hawkeye, BJ, Winchester, Margaret, Father Mulcahy, and Klinger.

155. Sergeant Yee.

156. He gave him a posthypnotic suggestion that whenever Yee felt like committing suicide he should twitch instead.

157. Colonel Potter and Colonel Daniel Webster Tucker.

158. A shot and a beer.

159. Aggie O'Shay.

160. As an example of meaningless, senseless destruction.

161. M*A*S*H NOTES.

162. "About Faces."

163. How to make New England Clam Chowder.

164. $22,312.

165. Major Van Zandt.

166. Private Jimmy Weston.

167. Being heard.

168. Hawkeye had kept a list of all the men BJ saved. He wanted it sent to Erin.

169. Klinger.

170. Someone once told Father Mulcahy that he wasn't worth a plugged nickel. This was Hawkeye's way of saying he was.

171. Margaret.

172. His purple bathrobe.

173. Potter.

174. Because Klinger's ex-wife had married his best friend.

175. The Presidential oath of office.

176. The British.

177. Klinger.

178. Winchester.

179. They both became orderlies.

180. They served the food in the mess tent.

181. "As Time Goes By."

182. Connie Izay, who had appeared in a number of episodes as a nurse.

183. Margaret.

184. Radar's teddy bear.

185. Rizzo.

186. A bottle of cognac.

187. A pair of boxing gloves.

188. Nurse Kelly

189. His black dress.

190. One of Henry's fishing flies.

191. The nurses' manual.

192. The hatchet.

During The Final Episode

1. "Goodbye, Farewell and Amen."

2. First, he drove his jeep through the wall of the Officers' Club and ordered a double bourbon (Hawkeye, of course, drank martinis). Then he wanted to operate on a patient without using an anesthetic, and accused the anesthetist of trying to smother the patient with the mask.

3. With a North Korean patrol nearby, Hawkeye had ordered a Korean woman to keep her baby quiet; instead, she panicked and smothered the child.

4. It was held at Inchon on the Fourth of July.

5. Guam.

6. Artie Jacobson.

7. Soon Lee Hahn.

8. All three were short and had black hair.

9. "Quintet in A for Clarinet and Strings."

10. Mozart.

11. All five were killed en route to a relocation center.

12. A mortar blast left him almost totally deaf.

13. Robert Pierpoint (who did, in fact, cover the Korean War for CBS news).

14. He was going to be a semiretired country doctor and a full-time Mr. Potter for Mrs. Potter.

15. Honolulu.

16. He was going to breed frogs for French restaurants in Louisiana.

17. To get to know his patients by being a small-town doctor back home.

18. To pigs; he was going to be a pig farmer.

19. The deaf.

20. She was going to work as a hospital nurse back in the States.

21. Chief of Thoracic Surgery at Boston Mercy Hospital. (This is another possible discrepancy with earlier episodes. Winchester had several times previously maintained that he had worked, and wanted to work again, at Massachusetts General.)

22. Margaret, who contacted her "Uncle" Bob Harwell, the Chairman of the Board at Boston Mercy.

23. He was going to marry Soon Lee and then remain in Korea to help her look for her family.

24. A copy of Elizabeth Barrett Browning's *Sonnetts From the Portuguese*.

25. An autographed picture of Klinger in his favorite dress.

26. They saluted him.

27. In a garbage truck.

28. The North Korean musicians.

29. Yellow.

30. By helicopter.

31. Colonel Potter gave her to a nearby orphanage.

32. "Good-bye, everybody. I'll pray for you."

33. BJ: "I'll see you back in the States. I promise. Just in case, I left you a note."
    Hawkeye: "What?"

34. "Good-bye."

35. The note he left was a large GOOD-BYE spelled out in rocks, which Hawkeye saw as he was leaving.

THE CHARACTERS

1. Benjamin Franklin Pierce.

2. The nickname was given to him by his father. Hawkeye was a character in James Fenimore Cooper's *Last of the Mohicans,* his father's favorite novel and supposedly the only book he ever read.

3. Crabapple Cove, Maine.

4. *Crabapple Cove Courier.*

5. He smelled it.

6. Daniel; he was a doctor also.

7. Early in the series, he mentioned that his mom was alive. Then later, all of a sudden, his dad became a widower.

8. No mention was ever made of any brothers, but, as with the above question, he did mention on a few occasions that he had a sister. Once she knit something for him and another time he told his dad to kiss mom and sis for him.

However, on several occasions he mentioned that he was an only child (probably just an oversight on the part of the show's writers).

9. Boston.

10. It stands simply for BJ (thus, there should not be any periods after the initials). He was named after his parents: his mother Bea and his father Jay.

11. Peg.

12. Erin (Mike Farrell's daughter, not coincidentally, is also named Erin).

13. July 1951.

14. Norma Jean; 16.

15. Stanford University.

16. Delta Phi Epsilon. (The same fraternity, by the way, which had blackballed Burns because he didn't have a blue serge suit.)

17. Leo Bardonaro.

18. Mill Valley, California.

19. 555-2757.

20. Waggles.

21. Twenty-eight.

22. Fort Sam Houston.

23. Sherman T. (He never said what the T. stood for.)

24. Mildred.

25. 42-36-42.

26. The date 8 September 1916 was mentioned in the "Point of View" episode. He also once said that he had been married on Groundhog Day (another probable oversight).

27. Hannibal, Missouri. (Once, however, he said he was going home to Nebraska.)

28. Classical Banjo.

29. Ebbe.

30. Stewart, Sheri Pershing, and Cory.

31. Tex Ritter.

32. Zane Grey.

33. On Guam, a still blew up in his face.

34. The cavalry.

35. Three. World Wars I and II, as well as Korea.

36. Sophie.

37. Methodist.

38. Bloomington, Illinois.

39. First, she was Mildred. Then, suddenly she became Lorraine (another probable oversight).

40. 36-24-34.

41. Andrew, Molly, and Jane.

42. University of Illinois.

43. He was the team's trainer.

44. Tanker Washington. (During one game, in the waning moments, Tank injured his ankle after carrying the ball to the one-foot line. Henry proceeded to tape the wrong ankle, for which Tanker shoots out Henry's porch light every year).

45. Marion.

46. Ferret face.

47. Louise.

48. Fort Wayne, Indiana.

49. Two; $30,000. ("I have two cars and a $30,000 house.")

50. "Rough and Ready."

51. Fort Benning, Georgia.

52. Charles Emerson Winchester III.

53. Boston.

54. 30 Briarcliff Lane.

55. Honoria, she stutters.

56. A tape-recorded letter.

57. Audrey Hepburn.

58. Harvard College; 1943.

59. Presbyterian.

60. A concert pianist.

61. Walter Eugene O'Reilly.

62. His ability to anticipate what is going to happen before it actually happens.

63. Ottumwa, Iowa.

64. Edna.

65. Ed.

66. Ottumwa Central.

67. Ranger.

68. Betsey.

69. Pokey.

70. Grape Nehi.

71. For the longest period of time he was, of course, a Corporal. In addition, for one show he was a "Corporal-Captain" and on another he was made a Lieutenant.

72. Electrolysis.

73. Maxwell Q. (It was never said what the "Q" stood for.)

74. Toledo, Ohio.

75. 1215 Michigan Avenue.

76. Toledo Mud Hens. (They are now a minor league team in the International League and affiliated with the Minnesota Twins.)

77. One.

78. Tony Packo's Cafe.

79. 1902 Front Street.

80. Hungarian hot dogs and sausages.

81. Lebanese.

82. He was Klinger's best friend until he married Klinger's exwife, Laverne.

83. Fort Dix, New Jersey.

84. Yvonne.

85. Butch.

86. Gus (or Gussie).

87. April 22nd.

88. Corporal, then Sergeant.

89. Hot Lips (the last two or three years of the show, out of growing respect for her, the nickname fell into disuse).

90. Alvin ("Howitzer") Houlihan.

91. "Forbidden Furlough."

92. "Over hill, over dale/Our love will never fail."

93. "Over hill, over dale/Our love will ever fail."

94. Eight months.

95. He called her his "little plebe."

96. John Patrick Francis.

97. His mother calls him Johnny, and his sister calls him Francis.

98. Padre.

99. Benedictine.

100. Angelica.

101. Girls' basketball at St. Mary's School

102. Saxophone.

103. Featherweight.

104. John Francis Xavier McIntyre.

105. Louise, Cathy, and Becky, respectively.

106. "Kid Doctor." (When he fought in the Intercamp Boxing Tournament.)

107. Honolulu.

108. Sergeant Pryor.

109. She was a nurse, and Henry's girlfriend during the first season.

110. Captain Sam Pak.

111. Luther.

112. Zola and Billy Bubba.

113. In charge of the motor pool.

114. Zelmo.

115. Hillda (with two "l"'s).

116. Brooklyn, New York.

117. In charge of supplies.

118. Brandon.

119. Sherry and ginger ale.

120. San Francisco.

121. Staminski.

122. He was The Swamp's houseboy during the first season.

123. Sam.

124. Milton Sidney Freedman.

125. He was a black surgeon during the first season.

126. He was the "gas passer" during the first season.

127. Bayliss.

QUOTATIONS

1. Major Freedman. (In fact, those were his last words in the final episode.)

2. Colonel Potter.

3. Major Burns.

4. Father Mulcahy.

5. Henry.

6. Radar. (Said when he was trying to impress a girl who loved classical music.)

7. Major Burns.

8. Hawkeye.

9. Major Winchester.

10. Hawkeye. (The usual beginning of one of his letters home.)

11. Hot Lips.

12. Major Burns. (Said to Nancy Sue Parker, Henry's young girlfriend.)

13. Colonel Potter.

14. Henry.

15. Hawkeye.

16. Corporal Klinger.

17. Major Burns.

18. The PA announcer.

19. Radar.

20. Henry. (One of his toasts.)

21. Hawkeye.

22. Colonel Potter.

23. Henry. (A comment he made about Captain Tuttle.)

24. Major Burns. (Said to Hawkeye.)

25. CBS newsman Robert Pierpoint. (Bringing to the 4077th, and to the world, news of the end of the war in the final episode.)

THE CAST

1. (e)	10. (o)	19. (p)
2. (j)	11. (v)	20. (n)
3. (t)	12. (z)	21. (r)
4. (i)	13. (w)	22. (c)
5. (m)	14. (y)	23. (l)
6. (g)	15. (q)	24. (h)
7. (q)	16. (u)	25. (s)
8. (d)	17. (b)	26. (k)
9. (x)	18. (a)	27. (f)

28. Gary Burghoff.
29. Alan Alda.
30. He has starred in eight, soon to be nine, TV series.
31. Robert Alda.

32. Elliott Gould. (The movie *M*A*S*H*), Wayne Rogers (the TV M*A*S*H), and Pernell Roberts (the TV show "Trapper John, M.D.")

33. William Christopher and Jamie Farr.

34. Gary Burghoff.

35. Alan Alda.

36. Karen Phillip.

37. They both attended Princeton and were both members of Princeton's famous Triangle Club.

38. McLean Stevenson.

39. Dr. Sam Marsh.

40. They had his Army cap bronzed, and then gave it to him.

41. William Christopher.

42. "City of Angels," a short-lived detective show.

43. Alan Alda.

44. Officer Bill Gannon.

45. McLean Stevenson.

46. Jamie Farr.

47. Mike Farrell.

48. Gary Burghoff.

49. Jamie Farr.

50. Michael Nicholson. He was editor of *Today's World* magazine, and Doris's boss.

51. He was George Plimpton, honorary quarterback for the Detroit Lions.

52. David Ogden Stiers.

53. Larry Linville.

54. Jamie Farr.

55. Wayne Rogers.

56. *Kill Me if You Can*.

57. McLean Stevenson, who was cousin Adlai's press secretary in the 1952 and 1956 campaigns.

58. Loretta Swit.

59. "The McLean Stevenson Show."

60. Gary Burghoff.

61. Jamie Farr.

62. "December Bride" and "Pete and Gladys."

63. "House Calls."

64. Alan Alda.

65. "The Tonight Show."

66. Both duplicated their movie roles of Radar and General Hammond for the TV series.

67. "We'll Get By."

68. Alan Alda—New York City; Mike Farrell—St. Paul, Minnesota; Wayne Rogers—Birmingham, Alabama; Harry Morgan—Detroit, Michigan; William Christopher—Evanston, Illinois; Jamie Farr—Toledo, Ohio; Larry Linville—Ojai, California; David Ogden Stiers—Peoria, Illinois.

69. 1. (e)   5. (f)
    2. (d)   6. (b)
    3. (g)   7. (h)
    4. (a)   8. (c)

70. 1. (j)   6. (e)
    2. (i)   7. (d)
    3. (h)   8. (c)

4.	(g)	9.	(b)
5.	(f)	10.	(a)

71. "The Chicago Teddy Bears."

72. "Grandpa Goes to Washington."

73. "Doc."

74. "In the Beginning."

75. "You'll Never Get Rich." (In an episode entitled "Bilko, the Art Lover.")

MASH: The Book

1. 1. (c)   3. (a)
    2. (d)   4. (b)

2. 1. (c)   3. (b)
    2. (d)   4. (a)

3. After being caught "in the act" by a train conductor, the woman Trapper was with yelled out, "He trapped me!"

4. "Me Lay."

5. He was a former javelin thrower. Someone gave him the name, the sports writers liked it, and it stuck.

6. Officially, it was Tent Number 6. Hawkeye named it The Swamp, which had also been the name of his apartment when he was in college.

7. The Double Natural.

8. Henry Blake.

9. Hamilton Hartington Hammond.

10. Black.

11. Captain.

12. Forty.

13. He was married! And he had two children (both boys).

14. He was single.

15. Benjamin Franklin Pierce, SR.

16. Trapper.

17. For safety reasons, choppers were not allowed to fly at night. If choppers flew that close to nightfall, at 6 o'clock, it meant that there were too many wounded to transport via ambulance. The 6 o'clock choppers meant a long night.

18. Thoracic surgery; he was called a "chest cutter."

19. Neurosurgery.

20. Jesus Christ.

21. $6,500.

22. James Lodge.

23. Henry and General Hammond.

24. Red Raiders.

25. They had a halfback who was second string with the Rams, and two tackles from the Browns.

26. 4077th.

27. "The sergeant from Supply and the Center from Nebraska."

28. 28 to 24.

29. Radar gave them his own version of their horoscopes. Henry gave them two bottles of scotch.

30. Midway Airport in Chicago.

31. Mary was his wife, and Billy, Stephen, and Karen were his children.

32. St. Lombard's.

33. Finestkind Clinic and Fish Market.

34. Lucinda Lively.

GUEST STARS

1. James Sikking.
2. Benjamin Franklin Pierce.
3. "Quincy."
4. Judy Farrell, Mike's wife.
5. Ron Howard.
6. Caryle Walton.
7. Radar's mom.
8. Elliott Carson.
9. "The Rockford Files."
10. Ed Flanders and Ed Begley, Jr., respectively.
11. Both appeared in the movie *Paper Lion*.
12. Marcia Strassman.
13. He played the part of Jack Sculley.

14. They are the two actors who played the part of Lieutenant Colonel Donald Penobscott.

15. Leslie Nielson.

16. Polaroid.

17. Tom Hartman.

18. Antony Alda, Alan's brother, and Robert Alda, his father.

19. Burt young.

20. "Trapper John, M.D."

21. She is the actress who played Nurse Leslie Scorch, Henry's girlfriend the first year.

22. Lary Wilcox.

23. Mako.

24. John Matuszak.

25. Pat Hingle.

26. Margaret's

27. Richard Masur.

28. Sam Fujiyama.

29. "Hill Street Blues."

30. Arlene Golonka.

31. "Temperatures Rising."

32. Robert Alda.

33. Arnold.

34. Susan St. James.

35. Tuttle. (The credits read, "Jonathan Tuttle as himself.")

36. Muldoon.

37. Colonel Maurice Hollister.

38. "Three's Company."

39. BJ's.

40. James Callahan.

41. "Hot L Baltimore."

42. Richard Benjamin and Paula Prentiss.

43. Goober Pyle.

44. Loudon Wainwright III.

45. Sal Viscuso.

M*A*S*H: THE MOVIE

1. Donald Sutherland was Hawkeye, and Elliott Gould was Trapper.

2. Duke.

3. Fred "The Hammer" Williamson.

4. Sally Kellerman was Hot Lips, and Jo Ann Pflug was Lt. Dish.

5. 1. (c)   5. (b)
   2. (e)   6. (g)
   3. (a)   7. (f)
   4. (d)

6. Walter K. Waldowski.

7. Lieutenant Dish.

8. Dago Red.

9. 1. (b)   4. (e)
   2. (c)   5. (f)
   3. (d)   6. (a)

10. With her tent bugged during one of her "meetings" with Burns in progress, she asked him to kiss her "hot lips."

11. After being taunted by Hawkeye, Burns attacked him. Burns was then put in a straightjacket and transferred out of the 4077th.

12. The Black Capsule.

13. They persuaded Lieutenant Dish to help him. (Disprove his homosexuality by sleeping with him.)

14. Yes.

15. He was a Congressman.

16. The 325th EVAC.

17. $5,000.

18. Spearchucker.

19. San Francisco 49ers.

20. Trapper, for the 4077th, and Jack Concannon, for the 325th.

21. The 4077th.

22. 18 to 16.

23. Goddamn (Goddamn army! Goddamn jeep! Goddamn war!, etc.) After editing for the television broadcast of the film, he just used "Damn" in its place.

24. They were given orally by the PA announcer.

25. "Tonight's movie has been *M*A*S*H*. Follow the zany antics of our combat surgeons as they cut and stitch their way along the front lines, operating as bombs and bullets burst around them, snatching love and laughter between amputations and penicillin."

26. Sally Kellerman.

27. *S*P*Y*S*.

ODDS & ENDS

1. Uijongbu.
2. "Best Care Anywhere."
3. "We Never Close."
4. Seoul City Sue.
5. Rosie's.
6. It was the tent of Hawkeye, et al.
7. 325th EVAC.
8. 98%.
9. 5428.
10. 5610.
11. 34.
12. 7033.
13. 6776.

14. 9412.

15. 4548.

16. 6133.

17. "Suicide is Painless."

18. Johnny Mandel.

19. 1. (d)   3. (a)
    2. (c)   4. (b)

20. Sunday night at eight (Eastern)

21. *Time* (16 October 1972). The review was written by Gerald Clarke.

22. Gene Reynolds.

23. "Lou Grant."

24. Twentieth Century Fox.

25. Stage 9.

26. Malibu Creek State Park in the Santa Monica Mountains.

27. Dr. Walter D. Dishell.

28. 46th place.

29. Jackie Cooper.

30. "Cheers."

31. "Mary Hartman, Mary Hartman."

32. The Pioneer Aviation episode entitled, "Mail Call."

33. Harry Morgan.

34. "Comrades in Arms" (Burt Metcalfe directed the first part and Alan Alda the second part).

35. "Ain't Love Grand."

36. "Chief Surgeon, Who?"

37. "The Interview."

38. Larry Gelbart.

39. The Scarlett O'Hara dress (a print chiffon in green and lavender), the Ginger Rogers dress (gold lamé), and the Carmen Miranda dress (a silver gown with a matching fruit-covered hat).

40. "Big Mac."

41. "Comrades in Arms."

42. McLean Stevenson.

43. "Sometimes You Hear the Bullet."

44. Mike Farrell.

45. "Mulcahy's War."

46. "Goodbye, Farewell, and Amen."

47. "Tuttle," "Iron Guts Kelly," "The Late Captain Pierce," "Foreign Affairs," "The More I See You," "Comrades in Arms," "In Love and War," "Fallen Idol," "The Party," "Inga," "Period of Adjustment," "Old Soldiers," "Sometimes You Hear the Bullet," "Sons and Bowlers," "Bless You, Hawkeye," "The Interview," "Dear Dad," "Dear Sigmund," "Point of View," "Life Time," "Hawkeye," "Dreams," and "Goodbye, Farewell, and Amen."

48. "As Time Goes By." (It was shown second to the last, but was the last to have been filmed.)

49. Henry Kissinger.

50. Former President Gerald Ford.

51. $450,000. (An all-time record.)

52. The "Who Shot J. R.?" episode of "Dallas."

53. Alan Alda and Loretta Swit.

54.. 250.

55. True. (It will be a part of the National Museum of American History.)

56. The George Foster Peabody Award.

57. "Making M*A*S*H."

58. WTTW.

59. Mary Tyler Moore.

60. "After M*A*S*H."

61. Harry Morgan, Jamie Farr, and William Christopher.

62. Robert Altman.

63. Ring Lardner, Jr.

64. Four.

65. Ring Lardner, Jr.

66. *Porkchop Hill*.

67. Gene Reynolds.

68.. Three asteriks. (One in between each of the letters.)

69. Richard Hooker.

70. Dr. Richard Hornberger.

71. He helped Hornberger write the book.

72. 8055th.

73. "Fix-'em, close-'em, and holler next."

74. Thirty-two successful free-throw baskets in a row.

75. A blue-and-white floral print Hawaiian shirt.

THE M*A*S*H EXAM

1. Berlinisha Polytechnisho.

2. Mildred, then Lorraine.

3. "Mississippi Mud"

4. The Statue of Liberty.

5. "Efficiency, punctuality, and bugling above and beyond the call of duty."

6. Benjamin Franklin Pierce.

7. Famous Las Vegas Writers' School

8. 98%.

9. 10½ C.

10. Frank Burns.

11. Vantz

12. Sergio Mendes and Brazil 66.

13. "Thanks."

14. Toledo Mud Hens.

15. Aggie O'Shay.

16. Radar's mom, Edna.

17. He touched his nose, and wouldn't admit it.

18. "Kid Doctor." (When he fought in the Boxing Tournament.)

19. McLean Stevenson.

20. The sorting of and allocation of treatment for the wounded according to a system of priorities designed to maximize the number of survivors.

21. "Quintet in A for Clarinet and Strings," K 581. (The first movement.)

22. Abigail Porterfield.

23. "Emotionally exhausted and morally bankrupt."

24. James Sikking.

25. BJ: "I'll see you back in the States. I promise. Just in case, I left you a note."
    Hawkeye: "What?"

Fun & Games from WARNER BOOKS

___**WORLD WAR II SUPER FACTS**
by Don McCombs and Fred L. Worth

(V30-157, $3.95)

This is a unique assemblage of little-known facts about World War II, chosen for their human interest and dealing with slang terms, nicknames, songs, lists, movie portrayals, key battles, military figures, and celebrities who took part in the vast panorama of the last global war.

___**THE COMPLETE UNABRIDGED SUPER TRIVIA ENCYCLOPEDIA**
by Fred L. Worth

(V30-513, $3.95)

Xavier Cugat's theme song? The bestseller of 1929? Miss Hungary of 1936? Here's more than 800 pages of pure entertainment for collectors, gamblers, crossword puzzle addicts and those who want to stroll down memory lane. It asks every question, answers it correctly, solves every argument.

___**THE COMPLETE UNABRIDGED SUPER TRIVIA ENCYCLOPEDIA, Volume II**
by Fred L. Worth

(V90-493, $3.95)

Okay, wise guy . . . so you think you know trivia, do you? Well, do you know which well-known TV actor directed the movie BEWARE! The BLOB? Sarah Barney Belcher's genealogical claim to fame? Muhammad Ali's aptly chosen CB handle? The presidential owner of Beans, the Boston bulldog? Which famous multimillionaire went down with the *Titanic*?

___**CELEBRITY TRIVIA**
by Edward Lucaire

(V95-479, $2.75)

Crammed with gossip galore, this book was written with the name dropper in all of us in mind. It's loaded with public and private memorabilia on actors, writers, rock stars, tyrants—and the scandalous facts they probably wouldn't want you to know. From Napoleon to Alice Cooper, anyone who has caught the public eye is fair game.

More *Mindbending* Books from WARNER